A Bible Prayer-Book for Today

Peter De Rosa was born in north London in 1932 and educated at the Jesuit College of St Ignatius. He read Philosophy and Theology at St Edmund's College and, having graduated from the Gregorian University in Rome, he lectured for five years at St Edmund's. He was Vice-Principal of Corpus Christi, London, an international institute for religious education, for five years, and is currently a radio producer.

A Bible Prayer-Book for Today

PETER DE ROSA

FONTANA/COLLINS

This book is for Francis
the answer to our prayers

First published in Fontana 1976
© Peter De Rosa 1976

Made and printed in Great Britain by
William Collins Sons & Co Ltd Glasgow

Table of Contents

Foreword

Christ, as we know from the gospels, was a man of prayer. He prayed because he needed prayer as much as he needed food and friendship and fresh air. Frequently his disciples must have found him in the early morning after a night spent in prayer, with the dew still glistening on his clothes and his face shining like the sun.

As a sincere Jew, Jesus naturally went to the Jewish scriptures to nourish his prayer-life. But he made those scriptures in a special way his own and brought them to the kind of fulfilment which only he was able to envisage.

In particular, when he prayed, he dared to call God 'Abba! My father!' This was an unprecedented venture of the human spirit. The Man who risked it never went back on the demands it made on him; he never for one moment failed in his obedience to God or in his love for his fellow men. And now that he has passed over to the Father, he never ceases to pray for us.

This book is made up of Bible Prayers. An Appendix shows how it can be used most effectively during the period of Lent and Easter.

Every author ambitiously – perhaps the right word is 'selfishly' – tries to kill as many birds with one stone as he can. My hope is that this book will be useful for private prayer and meditation as well as for public prayer in churches and school assemblies. With luck, even a hard-pressed clergyman or two may find it of assistance when preparing a last-minute sermon.

These are all Christian prayers, which means they are addressed to the Father of our Lord Jesus Christ and inspired with the confidence that Christ's Holy Spirit is praying in us. They are wholly based on the Old and New

Testaments. In fact, there are so many allusions in them to scripture it is quite impossible to give all the references. Today, when so many helpful books on prayer are being published, I wanted to write a prayer-book which relied exclusively on the only inspired source we Christians have, namely, the Jewish-Christian Bible.

Many Christians will be surprised not merely at the beauty but also at the fierceness and passion of many of the prayers. The surprise may well stem from the fact that we are far too selective in our reading of the Bible or we go on seeing things one-sidedly in the way we were taught to see them as children. The chief advantage of these prayers is this: they are so closely dependent on the Bible, we are again and again brought up with a jolt at the power, the acuteness, the sheer originality of the mind of Christ. They call us onwards 'to come up to the stature of the fullness of Christ' (Ephesians 4:13).

A Christian makes a point of always praying with, through and in Christ. 'He is always heard because he is so holy' (Hebrews 5:7). This is why we can be sure that when we ask the Father anything in Christ's name he will give it to us (John 15:16).

Part I

THE FATHER
OF OUR LORD
JESUS CHRIST

A Father who cares

Father, we know we are too anxious about our life,
   about what we shall eat or drink,
      and what we shall wear.
Your Son assured us that life is more than food,
   and the body more than clothing.
Turning to heaven, he said:
   'Look at the birds of the air;
   they neither sow nor reap nor gather into barns
      and yet your heavenly Father feeds them.
   Are you not of more value than they?
   However anxious you are,
      it will not add one second to your life.'
Turning to the earth, he said:
   'Why are you anxious about clothing?
   Look at the lilies of the field;
      see how they grow.
   They do not toil or spin, and yet I tell you,
   even Solomon in all his glory
      was not arrayed like one of these.
   And if God so clothes the grass of the field
      which is alive today
      and feeds the oven tomorrow,
   how much more will he clothe you,
      O men of little faith.'
The Man who taught us this
   ended his days on a cross,
      stranded between heaven and earth,
   without clothing and crying vainly for a drink.
And in this way, Lord, he showed you to be
   a Father who cares.

Maker of the world

Father, I acknowledge you are mystery to me
   and greater than all my thoughts.
This is why I turn to the world's wonders,
   praising you, their Maker.
My soul blesses you, Lord,
   and, in stillness, knows that you are God.
You are covered with sunlight
   as with a cloth of gold.
You have stretched out the heavens
   like a deep blue tent above our heads.
You make the clouds your chariot
   and ride on the wings of the wind.
The swirling wind is your messenger,
   and fire and flame your ministers.
You make springs gush in the valleys,
   telling them to flow between the hills.
You feed the birds of the air
   so they sing cheerfully.
You make the grass grow for the cattle
   and plants for man to cultivate
so he may win food from the earth:
   wine to gladden his heart
   oil to make his face shine
   bread to strengthen his arm.
Lord, though you are far, you are also very near.
Though you are mystery, you are as plain to me
   as sunlight and blue skies
   as clouds and fire and birdsong
     and a golden field of corn.

God is always there

Father, you have sifted me like sand
  and known me through and through.
You know when I sit down and when I stand up.
You know every thought of mine before I think it.
You know where I walk and when I lie down.
You know all the paths I'm going to take.
You know every word of mine
  before it finds its way on to my lips.
Wherever I turn, I find you facing me,
  and gently you lay your hand on me.
Father, how am I to fathom your thinking?
  It is far too high for me; I cannot.
Where can I go to elude your Spirit,
  where go to escape your presence?
If I scale the heavens you are there.
If I go to sleep in Hades you are there.
If I fly on sleepy morning's wings
  and dive into the depths of the sea,
even there your hand shall guide me
  and your right hand hold me.
If I call out to the darkness,
  'Cover me! Turn daylight into night!'
Even the darkness is not dark to you;
  night-time is bright as daytime,
  and dark is light to you.
Lord, it was you who knit me in my mother's womb
  and, before my birth, determined all my days.
I acknowledge you are fearful and wonderful;
  and I am thankful you are my Father.

God's great secret

Father, we thank you for the grace and peace
    you give to us in Jesus Christ.
Blessed are you,
    God and Father of our Lord Jesus Christ,
for in him you have given us every blessing
    and raised our earth-bound minds to heavenly things.
Before the world was made, Father,
    you chose us in him
    so that we should walk before him,
        holy as he is and blameless.
You destined us in love to be your dear children
    through Jesus Christ;
and this is why you poured out your grace upon us,
    poured it out without limit
    and without regard for our unworthiness
so that we might praise your goodness.
Father, we thank you for cleansing us
    and giving us a chance of a new kind of life
        in Christ who died for us.
Father, we thank you for making known to us
    a secret worthy of your infinite wisdom.
This plan, disclosed in Jesus Christ,
    is for the fullness of time.
It is a plan to unite all things
    in heaven and earth
        in Jesus Christ our Lord.
We unite our prayers with his, Father,
    so as to praise you for the charity of your love
        and to plead for your continuing help.

God's Word and the grass

Father, we are so different, you and I,
   I sometimes wonder what communion
      there can be between us.
I feel like a lonely sparrow on a roof-top.
My days are thin and pale as an evening shadow;
   I wither like the grass.
As for you, eternally tranquil God,
   you laid the earth's foundation,
   and the heavens were fashioned by your fingers.
They will all perish, but you remain.
They will all wear out like an old coat;
   and like an old coat you will cast them aside
      and don another.
But you, Lord, are always the same,
   and your years never fail.
I heard the voice the prophet heard when it said 'Cry!'
   but I said, 'What shall I cry?'
'Ah,' said the voice, 'all flesh is grass
   and all its beauty like the flowers of the field.
The grass withers, the flower fades,
   when the Lord's breath blows upon it.
Yes, all the people is grass;
   the grass withers, the flower fades.
But your Word, God, for ever stands.'
I thank you, Father, that, for all our frailty,
   you love us with an everlasting love.
You showed your love for us
   by sending your Son to be as we are,
   by sending your Word to become the flesh
      that is withering grass.

Where are the Everlasting Arms?

Father, there is a kind of suffering in the world
   before which most of us are forced to stand
      speechless, helpless and uncomprehending.
If we ourselves have never met a similar fate,
   how are we to understand the carnage of war,
   the instantaneous loss of all one's family
      in a fire or motor accident,
   the decimation of a village through an air-crash?
But we, too, are men;
   and ripples and echoes of their anguish reach us.
We feel for Job when he curses the day he was born.
May that day, he cries, be plucked out of the calendar.
May no woman ever again conceive upon that night.
May the stars of its dawn turn black
   and the eyelids of its morn stay shut for ever.
Man that is born of woman, Job laments,
   is of few days and full of trouble.
He blooms like a flower, then he withers;
   his life slides, glides away from him
      faster than a shadow.
Father, does it help the really desolate to be told
   that you, the eternal God, are their dwelling-place
      and underneath are the everlasting arms?
How kind you were and wise to send your Son
   to sweat blood in a Garden
   to feel the treacherous kiss of a friend upon his lips
   to cry out at his abandonment
   to die on arms that held up nothing
      but a body full of pain.

A Voice out of the whirlwind

Father, like Job we are full of questions.
We are puzzled and hurt
  by many of the things that happen to us
    and to those we love.
There is perhaps more merit in our vociferous complaints
  than in quiet, unbelieving acquiescence.
And yet, Father, we who cannot comprehend
    a single grain of sand
  are bound in the end
    to lay our finger on our lips.
In the bible story, you answered Job out of the whirlwind:
  'Who is this who stains wisdom with his foolish words?
Were you there when I laid
  the foundation of the world?
What does the earth rest on?
Who laid its corner-stone
  when all the morning stars in chorus sang
    and all God's sons were crying out for joy?
Did you give the Horse its might, those large, proud eyes?
Did you clothe in iron the Hippopotamus?
Do you not cringe before Leviathan, my Crocodile,
  whose sneeze is like the lightning water-borne
  whose eyes are like the eyelids of the dawn?'
Then Job confesses:
  'I have spoken what I did not understand;
  things too wonderful for me, which I did not know.'
Father, bear with my questions and complaints,
  for, while I know I must speak as I do,
  I do not doubt that, in the end,
    I, too, will bow my head in silent adoration.

The foolishness of God

Father, we humans pride ourselves on our achievements.
And we are rightly grateful to be living in this century,
   in these exciting times of film and television,
     of cars and jets and space exploration.
But we ask you, Lord, to teach us a higher wisdom
   and show us the standards we should live by.
How easy it is for us to think we are wise in everything,
   when really we are fools.
We thank you, God,
   for making foolish the wisdom of the world.
When the world, for all its wisdom,
   did not know you,
it pleased you, God,
   through the folly of what we preach
     to save all who believe.
Jews, Paul says of his contemporaries, seek miracles;
   non-Jews dabble in philosophy.
For our part, we preach Christ crucified.
To Jews this was a stumbling-block,
   to non-Jews folly;
but to those who have been called,
   both Jews and non-Jews,
Christ the power of God,
Christ the wisdom of God.
We thank you, God, for your foolishness,
   so much wiser than men;
and for your weakness,
   so much stronger than men.

The Father always answers prayer

Father, your Son has said without reserve,
  'Whatever you ask the Father in my name,
    he will grant it.'
How is it, then, we ask and you grant us nothing,
  and do not even seem to hear us?
Is it, Father, because we do not always know
  what we are really asking for?
In the garden of Gethsemane Christ said,
  'Father, let this chalice pass me by,
  but not as I will but as thou wilt.'
For you, God, are a kind and understanding Father.
When a son asks his father for bread,
  he will not give him a stone.
But neither when a son asks for a stone,
  will he give him a stone.
When a son asks his father for a fish,
  he will not give him a snake.
But neither when he asks for a snake,
  will he give him a snake.
If earthly fathers give good gifts to their children
  even when they ask for things
    which would do them harm,
how much more will you, good Father,
  give us what is good for us?
Only on this understanding is Christ's saying true:
  'Ask and you will receive;
  seek and you will find;
  knock and the door will be opened to you.
  For everyone who asks receives,
  and he who seeks finds,
  and to him who knocks
    the door will be opened.'

God of labyrinths

Father, Jesus seems never to have tired of saying:
  Everyone who exalts himself will be humbled,
  but he who humbles himself will be exalted.
The Pharisee, in his story,
  stood in the synagogue in silent prayer.
His whole life was a Lenten exercise.
He thanked you, God, as he supposed,
  for his fasts, his many efforts to be good,
   for his not being a sinner like the rest of men,
    and plainly not at all like yonder publican.
The publican, for his part, stood a long way off,
  seeing no one and not knowing he was seen.
He did not even dare to lift his eyes to heaven,
  but only beat his breast and said,
  'O God, be merciful to me a sinner.'
My heart is drawn irresistibly
  to that humble publican
   whom Christ exalted.
My only fear is, Father, I may end up as a Pharisee
  who believes himself to be a publican and says:
'I thank you, God, I am not like the rest of men
  who do not know that they are sinners.
I thank you especially for not being like
  the Pharisees surrounding me.
I do not keep the commandments,
  neither do I pray or fast or give alms;
but I stand far apart in church
  not daring to lift my eyes to heaven.
And I beat my breast continuously and say:
  "Oh God, be merciful to me a sinner." '
O God of labyrinths,
  be merciful to me
   a Pharisee.

The God who does nothing

Father, we are told that half the world is hungry.
Many will pray to you today,
　'Our Father . . . give us this day our daily bread',
and no manna will fall on them from scorching skies.
Many will pray to you today,
　'Lord, our fields are thirsty,
　　our people are famine-stricken,
　please send rain upon our land',
and no rain will fall on their land today
　or tomorrow or a hundred tomorrows.
Fathers will plead with 'the Father of Mercies'
　for their swollen-bellied children,
and no help will come from God or men,
　so they will feel
　　both earth and heaven have rejected them.
Lord, I do not know why so many are hungry and thirsty.
I turn to Christ on his cross and find no comfort there.
He, too, has the look of someone
　whose prayers are never answered,
　compatriot of those who live in bone-dry lands.
He grew up before you, God, like a young plant
　and like a root out of dry ground.
In him I find no form or loveliness.
He has no beauty that I should desire him.
I see but one more Man who feels rejected and despised;
　and not by men only but by God his Father, too.
Father, with the desiccated Christ I pray,
　Give them bread, send rain upon their lands.
Lord, I do not know why so many are hungry and thirsty,
　only that the little I could do
　　I do not do.

The Father who is Light

Father, I believe that you are Light
   and in you there is no darkness at all.
I believe that you are Love
   and in you there is no hatred or revenge.
Your love was shown to us
   when you made us your children in Jesus Christ.
When his face shines on us
   we know the darkness is passing away
     and the light is already shining.
Father, whoever says he is in light and hates his brother
   is, for all his eloquence, still in darkness.
It is the man who cares for his brother
   who is living in light.
Such a one will never stumble or lose his way,
   for the darkness has been lifted from his eyes.
Father, keep us always in your light and love
   and help us walk confidently in the light.
It was your love that awakened love in us.
We only love because you loved us first.
Drive from our hearts the hypocrisy that says,
   'I love you, God',
     when all the time we hate or despise each other.
That is a lie we keep repeating even in our prayers.
If we do not love the brother whom we see,
   how can we love you, God,
     whom we have never seen?
Show me again, Father, that in loving you,
   I am loving my brethren,
and in loving my brethren,
   I am loving you.

Part II

CHRIST IN HIS MINISTRY

The tempting of Christ

Father, as soon as Jesus was baptized
    your Spirit drove him into the wilderness.
There you spoke to his heart.
For forty days and nights he was alone with you,
    neither eating nor drinking.
Like Israel, whose Saviour and Christ he was,
    he had to be tempted and tried.
Nothing distracted him from communion with you
    in the Holy Spirit,
neither the burning sun by day,
    nor the frigidity and prowling beasts of night.
At the end of his fast,
    he looked like a root out of the desert ground,
    without form or any beauty.
Then came the Tempter, whispering in the wind:
    'Turn the desert stones into bread.
    Float down from the pinnacle of the temple
        to be borne aloft on angels' wings.
    Bow down and worship me
        and yours will be all the kingdoms of the world.'
But in his ear, Jesus heard your voice, Father,
    'This is my beloved Son',
and in his heart he felt the beating
    of the Dove's white wings.
'Satan, begone,' he said through black, parched lips,
    'Thou shalt not tempt the Lord thy God.'
When he opened his eyes,
    there were pools of water in the wilderness;
and the world's salvation, for all the agony to come,
    already was assured.

The baptism of Christ

Father, when your Son's long preparation was over,
  he took his place among wrong-doers
    on the banks of the river Jordan.
When his turn came,
  he was baptized by John the Baptist.
He was immersed in the waters
  as though he were unclean
    like the rest of men.
I thank you, Father, for the humility of Christ
  who became so one with sinners
    that he underwent this sign of purification.
He is the Saviour
  and he felt he had to be one with his people
    in their sense of estrangement,
    in their need of cleansing.
Afterwards, you confirmed him, Father, as your Son:
  'This is my beloved Son.
  I am very pleased with him.'
Then over the waters, as if it were a new Genesis,
  your Spirit descended
  dove-like
  gentle pure and radiant
and anointed him for his future mission of peace.
Father, I thank you
  for the white dove-like soul of Christ
  who, from the first, became
    your Servant and our Servant.
I pray that I, too, may be faithful to my baptism
  by showing the obedience of a child
    and becoming, like Christ, an envoy of your peace.

Christ goes home to Nazareth

Father, when Christ returned home to Nazareth,
  he went to the synagogue on the Sabbath day.
When he was asked to read,
  he chose this passage from Isaiah:
'The Spirit of the Lord is upon me,
  because he has anointed me
    to preach good news to the poor.
He has sent me to preach release to captives
  and recovery of sight to the blind,
to set at liberty those who are oppressed,
  and to proclaim the acceptable year of the Lord.'
Then Jesus closed the book saying:
  'Today in your hearing this scripture is fulfilled.'
Father, I thank you for anointing Christ with the Spirit
  to preach good news to me.
For I am poor and have no spiritual resources
  except for those Christ gives me.
I am a captive to my own desires
  and cannot find release
    unless Christ flings open my prison door.
I am blind and hopelessly lost
  unless Christ who is the Light of the world
    comes and shows me the Way.
I am oppressed within by many tyrannies,
  by false ambitions, laziness and greed;
and how can I find release, Father,
  unless Christ the Servant,
    the only fully liberated Man,
  comes to me and sets me free?

Christ the Good Shepherd

Father, there is no lovelier psalm than this:
   'The Lord is my shepherd, I shall not want;
     he makes me lie down in green pastures.
   He leads me beside still waters;
     he restores my soul.
   He leads me in the paths of righteousness
     for his own name's sake.'
Father, I am glad you are a watchful shepherd.
Through Jeremiah, you said,
   'He who scattered Israel will gather him,
   and he will keep him as a shepherd keeps his flock.'
Through Ezekiel, you said,
   'The shepherds of Israel have been feeding themselves.
   My sheep were scattered over all the face of the earth.
   Behold, I, I myself will search for my sheep
     and will seek them out.
   And I will set up over them one shepherd,
     my servant, David, and he shall feed them.'
Father, the one shepherd you have given us is
   Jesus Christ, your Son and David's son.
He said, 'I am the Good Shepherd.
   I know my own and my own know me.
   I lay down my life for the sheep.'
Father, we thank you for shepherding us
   in Christ Jesus, a shepherd who is faithful and true.
He died for us, but he is alive for ever;
   and, though once we were lost,
he has gathered us up again,
   and no one shall snatch us from his arms.

Christ's love of the sick

Father, today our hearts turn to those who are sick.
We are all limbs of Christ's body
  so that if one limb suffers, all suffer together.
Those who are sick have a special cross to bear:
  they are called to witness that the love of Christ
    can turn even suffering into joy.
Christ himself was devoted to the sick.
At sundown, the sick were brought to him
  so that the whole city
    seemed to be gathering at his door.
And he laid his hands on every one of them;
  and many were healed because they trusted him.
Jesus was willing, against bitter opposition,
  to heal even on the Sabbath day.
The honest needs of the sick, he claimed,
  took priority over the Jewish holy day.
'The Sabbath was made for man, not man for the Sabbath.'
Father, I thank you
  for the gentle healing hands of Christ
  who came as Physician to a sick world.
And I pray with him for all who have to endure
  loneliness and pain
  envy of those healthier than themselves
  the agonizing difficulties of prayer.
And if, from time to time, they lose heart,
  strengthen them, Father, with Christ's Holy Spirit
  so that they know no one has failed too much
    if he is still trying not to fail.

The Transfiguration of Christ

Father, today we recall what happened on a hill.
Jesus took Peter, James and John with him;
  and there, on a rocky height,
  he was transfigured.
No launderer ever made clothes so white.
And there appeared in Jesus' glow
  Elijah, most renowned of prophets,
  and Moses who gave Israel her law.
Peter, foolish and unthinking, said:
  'Master, we are glad we came.
  We'll make three arbours here, one for each of you.'
From the cloud above them, Father, your voice came:
  'This is my beloved Son; listen to him.'
And when the disciples looked,
  they saw no one but Jesus.
Father, I thank you for this gospel story
  which illustrates so well Christ's sovereignty.
I believe, Lord, that in everything he says and does
  he lights up and fulfils the law and the prophets;
  and it is enough now to listen to him.
For Jesus is your Christ,
  even though death and dereliction
    are waiting for him in Jerusalem.
It will be dark there,
  and on another hill, shaped like a skull,
  two other men will be beside him.
From his unclothed body no light will radiate;
  and even you, Father, will be silent,
except for the one Word you will be saying to us
  in the tremendous love of Jesus crucified.

The unfathomable Christ

Father, I suppose it's no use our complaining
   Christ's message is a crucifixion,
     seeing he promised us nothing else.
Before Christ came, it was said,
   'An eye for an eye and a tooth for a tooth.'
That, people agreed, was an excellent balance of justice.
While it is wrong to take two eyes for one,
   it seemed no less unjust to allow a criminal
     to take one eye without punishing him.
But Christ knew you well enough, Father, to say:
   'Do not resist one who is evil.
   But if anyone strikes you on the right cheek,
     turn to him the other cheek as well;
   and if anyone is keen to take your coat,
     let him have your overcoat as well;
   and if anyone bullies you into going one mile,
     go with him an extra mile.'
Father, I have flipped through the gospels so often
   and heard so many stories of 'Jesus meek and mild',
I sometimes forget that Christ is unfathomable,
   that his teaching turns the world on its head.
I pray, Father, that I may not get so used to him
   that I transform him into an idol,
   his cross into an ornament,
   his gospel into a children's fairy tale.
And if this has not happened to me already,
   why do I class his message as impractical,
when I know that it was only by him practising it
   that he redeemed the world?

The courtesy of Christ

Father, I marvel at the patience
  and the courtesy of Christ.
The disciples had been with him many months
  and seen at first hand his humility.
Then, at this late stage, James and John take him aside
  to ask him for a favour.
'Grant us to sit,
  one at your right hand and one at your left
    in your glory.'
Jesus said: 'You do not know what you are asking.
  Can you drink the cup I am to drink
  or be baptized with the baptism
    with which I am to be baptized?'
They answered yes, and Jesus added:
  'Indeed, the cup I am to drink you, too, will drink.
  With my baptism you, too, will be baptized.
  But to sit at my right hand or at my left
    is not mine to grant.
  That belongs to those for whom it is prepared.'
The other disciples were angry with James and John,
so Jesus called them to him and said:
  'The rulers of the pagans lord it over them.
  It must not be like that with you.
  Whoever wants to be great among you
    must be your servant;
  whoever wants to be first among you
    must be everybody's slave.
  For the Son of Man came not to be served but to serve,
    and to give his life so many can go free.'
Father, I thank you for Christ's exquisite courtesy
  in entrusting the gospel to disciples
  in whom I see all the failings
    I am aware of in myself.

B.P. B.T. — B

The ferocious love of Christ

Father, I treasure most the picture of Christ
  as a man brim-full of compassion.
Did he not take pity on the crowds
  because they were like sheep without a shepherd?
But his compassion was in no way soft;
  it had about it that divine ferocity
    out of which sprang the world.
This is why we need at times to picture him
  as the Warrior, Faithful and True,
  seated on a white charger.
His eyes are like a flame of fire,
  and on his head are many diadems.
He is clad in a robe dipped in blood,
  and his name is the Word of God.
The armies of heaven ride after him,
  arrayed in white and seated on white horses.
And from his mouth a sharp sword comes
  with which he is to smite the nations.
He will rule them with a rod of iron;
  and he will tread the wine-press of the fury
    of the wrath of God the Almighty.
Upon his robe and thigh he has a name inscribed,
  'King of Kings and Lord of Lords.'
Father, I thank you for reminding me
  of the strength of the love of the compassionate Christ.
For he who had pity on the multitude
  never relented in his demand
    that they leave everything for the kingdom's sake
  and take up their cross
    and follow him.

The anger of Christ

Father, Christ warned us severely against the anger
   which is the little brother of death.
It was said of old:
   'Whoever murders is liable to judgement.'
But Jesus said:
   'Whoever is angry with his brother is liable to judgement.'
All the same, there were times, Father,
   when Christ himself was smouldering with anger.
Once, the Pharisees were watching to see if,
   on the Sabbath and in the synagogue,
   he would dare to heal a man with an arthritic hand.
He asked them: 'Is it lawful to do good or to do harm,
   to save life or to kill?'
Their silence made him round on them with anger,
   grieved at the hardness of their hearts.
He was astounded that they could not see their blasphemy.
For, in the name of God and of his law,
   they thought it holier
      to prefer cruelty to kindness.
The Pharisees were only waiting to pounce on him.
Jesus knew it, but healed the man with the arthritic hand.
He did not hesitate to let himself
   be accused of kindness even on the Sabbath day,
and to choose life and health
   though it incited them to thoughts of murdering him.
Father, Christ has said that we must never yield
   to an unloving anger towards our brothers,
but he has shown as well
   that there must always be a deadly conflict
      between light and darkness
      between a righteous and an unrighteous wrath.

Christ's onslaught on hypocrisy

Father, I marvel at Christ's soul,
 as limpid as fresh water in a stream.
How vehemently your Holy One reacted to hypocrisy.
How he slated those who did not practise
 what they preached.
'Woe to you, scribes and Pharisees, hypocrites!' he cried.
'You slam the kingdom of heaven against men,
 neither entering yourselves,
  nor letting others enter.'
They cared so scrupulously for man-made trivia
 and wholly forgot the weightier matters of religion:
 justice, mercy, faith.
'Guides without eyes,' he called them,
 'putting mosquitoes through a sieve
  and swallowing camels whole.
Woe to you, scribes and Pharisees!
 you look like whitewashed sepulchres
 which appear outwardly beautiful
 but inside are piled to the roof with dead men's bones.
And you,' he added, 'are stacked with evil and hypocrisy!'
Father, I know that Christ would have us seem
 no more or less than what we are.
If we are evil, he wants us to be evil openly
 so that good is not compromised or contaminated
  by its association with us.
Help me, Father, to see that Christ is just as vehement
 at the pharisaism he detects in me today.
Help me to practise what I preach, so that, at least,
 I do not ask anything more of others
  than I am prepared to do myself.

The Man who threatens with fire

Father, Isaiah the prophet speaks with brutal frankness
   of the fate of sinners who rebel against you.
Their corpses will be thrown into the city's incinerator:
   their worm shall not die;
    their fire shall not be quenched.
Jesus had no less an aversion to iniquity.
Whoever causes scandal, he said, to a little one
   who believes in me,
it would be better for him
   if a great millstone were hung around his neck
    and he were thrown into the sea.
Jesus adopts Isaiah's imagery of perpetual fire:
   If your hand leads you into sin, cut it off.
   Far better to enter life maimed than to go
    two-handed into unquenchable fire.
For hell is that incinerator
   where the worm does not die
    and the fire is not quenched,
   where evil-doers are pickled with fire.
Father, Jesus chose to speak in this prophetic way
   only because he loves us passionately
    and wants to keep us from harming others
    and ourselves.
His words no longer make it possible for me to think
   that evil is not *so* evil
   that scandal to others is not so savage after all
   that I will easily be pardoned
    because I spoke or acted unreflectingly.
Father, Jesus loves us in the way you love us;
   which is why he insists we take responsibility
    for all the evil that we do
and stand prepared, if we are rubbish,
   to be burned like rubbish.

The Man who threatens with mercy

Father, I am nearly always angry when someone judges me.
What can anyone know, I roar inwardly,
    about why I acted in this or the other way?
Can anyone else think himself inside my skin,
    inside the crannies of my skull?
I am even angrier when a person harshly judges
    someone close to me whom I love and revere.
How outraged my soul is that some stranger,
    without knowledge or sympathy, sensitivity or insight,
        should dare to criticize my friend.
And yet, Lord, I myself behave like a circuit judge,
    holding my Assizes wherever I go.
On the flimsiest hearsay evidence I am prepared
    to sentence and condemn a fellow human being.
He has no need or even the opportunity to speak
    but I am sure I know him through and through.
Father, Jesus, threatening us with infinite mercy, said:
    'Judge not and you will not be judged.
    Whatever judgement you mete out to others,
    that same judgement will be meted out to you.'
Lord, this is the best or worst bargain
    that Jesus ever struck with us.
If I avoid judging my brothers,
    I will evade your judgement, God.
If I forgive them,
    I will be forgiven.
But if I treat others brutally,
    I will be treated like that brute I have become.
I pray, Father, that I may so live that when I die
    I will find myself to be
        a very gentle and forgiving judge.

The Man who came to call sinners

Father, Jesus was only prepared to give his foes one sign
   and that was the sign of Jonah.
He meant the preaching of repentance
   even to hardened sinners;
    the offer of God's free pardon to everyone.
In the bible story, Jonah was very annoyed with God
   for asking him to preach repentance
    to the hated Ninevites.
The Ninevites had responded to his preaching
   with fasting and penance
   and thereby won the forgiveness of God.
'I knew,' the prophet angrily complained,
   'that you are a gracious God and merciful,
   slow to anger and overflowing with steadfast love.'
Father, the message and irony of that story
   had eluded many of Jesus' listeners.
They angrily complained that he was eating
   with publicans and women of the street.
If he were really a holy man, they said,
   he would not be so interested in sinners.
Jesus added to the Book of Jonah an irony of his own.
He said to his detractors:
   'The healthy do not need a doctor,
    only those who are sick.
   I came to call not righteous people
    but sinners.'
Father, help me read aright the only sign Christ gives:
   his merciful love of outcasts and sinners.
For his love, Father, is the perfect parable
   of the love you have for us,
    a love which extends to all sick, unrighteous people
     of whom I am the first.

Jesus guest and host

Father, when Jesus entered the house of Simon the Pharisee
  he was grieved that Simon offered him
      no water to wash the road-stains from his feet
      no welcoming kiss
      no oil to anoint his head
      no ointment to anoint his feet.
It was left to a woman of the streets
    to wash his feet with her tears
    to honour them with her kisses
    to anoint them with the costly ointment
        she had bought.
Simon must only have invited Jesus out of curiosity.
No doubt he despised Jesus for being a friend of sinners.
Jesus, in turn, was hurt by Simon's inhospitality.
He was a Jew and deeply valued
    the traditional courtesies offered to the stranger.
There is a saying: My house is your house.
Teach us, Father, to be more generous
    in opening the door of our house to others
    in sharing the joys of our hearth and home
        with friends and passing strangers.
Help us to be magnanimous hosts
    so that others may share in whatever domestic joy
        you have given us.
Jesus showed, Father, that you and he
    are very generous hosts.
He said to his disciples just before he went away:
    'Do not be upset at my departure.
    In my Father's house there are many rooms.
    If it were not so, would I have said,
    I am going to prepare a place for you?'

Part III

CHRIST IN HIS SUFFERING

The Man on a donkey

Father, there was more love than bitterness
  in Christ's lament over the Jewish capital:
   'O Jerusalem, Jerusalem, stoning the prophets
    and killing those who are sent to you!
  How often would I have gathered your children
    as a hen gathers her chicks underneath her wings,
     and you would not.'
Small wonder, Father, that on that shining day
  when palms were waved and loud hosannas sung,
  the canny Carpenter from Nazareth
    did not allow himself to be deceived.
As he rode slowly down Mount Olivet,
  sitting meek and lowly on an ass,
the crowds of his disciples cried,
  'Blessed be the king
    who comes in the name of the Lord!
  Peace in heaven and glory in the highest.'
But Christ could not cry peace when there was no peace.
The nodding donkey kept reminding him of his resolve,
  made in the desert long ago,
  to serve God and his fellows in humility.
As he approached Jerusalem
  and saw the city of peace he so much loved,
he wept over it and said:
  'If only you knew, even at this late hour,
  the things that would bring you peace.'
But they did not know, Father,
  and I too frequently forget,
that this Man on his donkey is our peace:
  this meek One to whom you gave the land,
  this lowly One whom you exalted.

Christ is condemned for heresy

Father, I bless you for the fortitude of Christ.
He had no official role among his people,
    being a layman, not a priest or scribe or elder.
He, nonetheless, obeyed your word, Father,
    even though it brought down on his head
        the wrath of the religious establishment.
To them he spoke with defiant irony this parable:
    'A man planted a vineyard, hedged it,
    dug a wine-press round it, built a tower,
    then, hiring it out to tenants, went abroad.
    At harvest-time, he sent his servant
        to collect his dues.
    The tenants beat him and sent him away empty-handed.
    Again and again this happened till the owner said:
    "One servant I have left, my beloved son.
    Him will I send, they'll surely honour him."
    But no. They said: "This is the heir.
    We'll kill him and then claim the inheritance."
    Taking the son, they threw him out of the vineyard,
        killing him.
    What,' said Jesus, 'will the owner of the vineyard do?
    He'll come and slaughter them
        and hire the vineyard out to other men.'
Father, your Son was thrown out of the vineyard of Israel
    and put to death for heresy.
I pray for religious leaders for whom religion is routine
    instead of a hunger and thirst for you,
and who, in your name, persist in crucifying Christ.
I pray for all of us who do not know that truth
    is like light, a continuous gift no one can own,
    and like life which we can only save
        by losing it.

A beautiful thing

Father, only Jesus grasped the greatness of the work
    you had given him to do.
But those of his followers who loved him
    sensed in him a quality that excited them
        to acts of special honour and devotion.
Such a person was the woman
    with the alabaster jar of ointment of pure nard.
Entering the house of Simon the leper at Bethany,
    she broke the jar
    and poured the precious ointment over Jesus' head.
Some said indignantly: 'This is a waste.
    This costly ointment could have been sold
    and all the proceeds given to the poor.'
But God's Anointed sprang to her defence:
    'Leave her alone; why do you trouble her?
    She has done a beautiful thing to me.
    The poor are with you always
    and any time you wish you can do good to them.
    But you will not always have me.
    She did what she was able to do,
    and anointed my body in advance for its burial.'
Then Jesus added: 'Truly, I say to you,
    wherever in the whole world the gospel is preached,
        what she has done will be told in memory of her.'
Father, Jesus so admired spontaneous, generous love
    he gratefully turns this woman's simple act of kindness
        into a memorial as everlasting as the Eucharist.
For in one brief moment, never to be forgotten,
    she prophetically anoints a Jesus doomed to die
        as the Christ of God.

They betrayed each other

Father, Jesus was to be spared nothing in his passion,
   not even betrayal by a trusted friend.
Like Jesus himself,
   Judas could read the signs of the times
   and realized before the rest that Jesus had to die.
Judas had signed on for triumph not disaster;
   and yet the kingdom, he saw, was not to be restored.
Jesus was the eternal provincial, still surrounded
   by the riff-raff from the streets
   and a motley crowd of untalented disciples
     with hardly a sword among them!
He had come riding into the capital
   not on a prancing war-horse but on a donkey
     as if making war on war and fun of revolutions.
In Bethany, he even spoke
   of being anointed for his burial.
Why should Judas scruple to betray this Man
   who had betrayed him first so shamelessly?
Jesus, he knew, had healed the blind, the sick, the lame;
   but who could doubt that when the test came
   he would not defend himself or Israel's cause
     but go meekly like a sheep to the slaughter?
Father, of all the figures in the passion story,
   I feel the closest affinity to Judas.
Christ troubles and overturns too much in me,
   my hopes and dreams, my standards, my ambitions,
so that I, too, begin to think with Judas my brother
   that the world is better rid of him,
   that it would have been better for us all
     if he had never been born.
Father, do not lead Jesus into temptation,
   nor let him fall repeatedly
     into the hands of his friends.

Their last meal together

Father, on Holy Thursday,
  we recall the day when your Holy One
    gave himself to sinners to make them holy.
Rising from table, and clad only in a towel,
  he washes his disciples' feet.
He has come, Father, to serve, not to be served.
With this prophetic gesture,
  he looks forward to the morrow when,
  stripped like a slave,
  he is to die upon the cross
    to prove his love for his friends.
Later at supper, Jesus takes bread,
  This is my body, he says. Eat.
And taking a cup of wine,
  This is my blood. Drink.
With this prophetic gesture,
  he gives himself into his disciples' hands.
He hands himself over to his friends
  before Judas, another friend,
    can hand him over to his enemies.
This is my life given for you, he is saying,
  in this secret yet stupendous act
    of self-betrayal.
At this moment, Jesus knows there is no turning back.
He has given himself away completely;
  he is broken and distributed.
Father, we pray that not even death shall sever
  the bond between Christ and those he loves
  in this sacrament of the breaking of the bread.

One Leper who gives thanks

Father, of the ten lepers Jesus cured,
  only one returned to give him thanks;
  only one remembered.
In this story I see an image
  of my own ungrateful and forgetful self.
Lord, you have given me life and love and friends,
  and yet, at best, only once in ten times do I return
    to offer you my thanks.
You have given me, too, the priceless gift of health.
A millionaire with ulcers or heart trouble
  is not nearly as rich as I.
Yet I can awake each morning over many years
  without pain
    and radiant with health,
and though I could reach you
  with but a glance of my heart
    I do not remember to say thank you.
But, Father, in this splendid gospel story
  I also see an image of Christ
    who became as a leper for our sakes.
On the night before he died, he gave you thanks
  and broke himself in pieces,
    asking thus to be remembered.
And at the resurrection you cleansed your Christ;
  you made him white and whole again
    in the baptismal waters of the Spirit.
And now, Father, at every Eucharist,
  we join the Leper whom you cleansed
in a sacred meal which guarantees
  that whatever else may vanish from the world
    his gratitude to you will never cease.

Before cock-crow

Father, when Jesus sensed his hour was at hand,
  he went with his disciples to Mount Olivet.
'You will all fall away,' he said, 'for it is written:
"I will strike the shepherd
  and the sheep will be scattered." '
Peter said, 'The rest may fall away but I will not.'
And Jesus replied:
  'Peter this very night before cock-crow,
  three times you will deny me.'
'No, Lord,' cried Peter, 'I would die with you
  but I will not deny you.'
Then he who had lifted his head and boasted like a cock
  nodded and slept three times in Gethsemane.
When Judas came with an armed guard to arrest his Master,
  Peter, with all the rest, ran off into the night.
Soon afterwards, in the courtyard,
  Peter denied his Master three times
    at the taunt of a serving maid.
While he was still uttering his oath,
  the cock began to crow.
And the Lord turned to Peter and looked at him;
  and Peter remembered his words,
  'Before cock-crow three times you will deny me.'
And he went out and wept bitterly.
Father, teach me, through Peter's humiliation,
  to realize I am always weaker than I think.
Give me the light and strength of your Spirit
  to resist temptation
  to repent like Peter immediately I fall
and to know that Christ whom I repeatedly deny
  is always looking at me
  ready to forgive me
    unto seventy times seven.

The Man who humbled himself

Father, you know how proud we are;
    so full are we to the brim with self-importance
        there is no room for you at all.
Sometimes we are so proud
    we pride ourselves on our supposed humility.
Most of the troubles in this world are caused
    by those of us who think too highly of ourselves.
We have no desire to serve others,
    preferring to be served by *them*.
Jesus, by contrast, came to serve, not to be served.
In his own eyes, Father, he was your Unprofitable Servant.
This is why he never acted out of selfishness,
    why there was not the slightest conceit in him,
    why he took the lowest place at your table.
Help us, Lord, through his example,
    to begin to think others better than ourselves.
Give us the mind of Christ who,
    though he was one with you, God,
    did not count his equality with you
        something to hold on to at all costs.
No, Lord, he poured himself all away.
He took the form of a slave
    and was born like any other man.
And being a man, he humbled himself,
    becoming obedient to death,
        even to a slave's death on a cross.
We thank you, Father, for exalting him for his humility
    and giving him the name above all names,
        your own name 'Lord'.

The day he died

Father, in sympathizing with Christ on his cross
    we are sympathizing with suffering people everywhere.
We are joining our prayers to the prayers of
    the hungry and the thirsty
    the hurt and the lonely
    the sick and the dying
    the outcasts and the refugees.
We are uniting ourselves with
    all who are oppressed
    all the known innocents who are condemned to death
    all who are betrayed by their friends.
We are sharing in the pain of
    all who are adjudged fools
        by the people they have served all their lives
    all who are nailed to the cross
        of other men's sins and stupidities
    all who feel in their hearts
        that you, God, have abandoned them.
We believe that Jesus Christ, your Son,
    is also the Son of Man.
We believe that in him all mankind
    has suffered, been humiliated and died.
But we are confident too
    that by his bruises all of us are healed.
This is why, Father, we take our place
    at the foot of his cross,
knowing that Good Friday is really good
    because of him who loved us
        and gave himself up for us.

The Man who is attached to his cross

Father, when Jesus was nailed to his cross,
    the crowds below kept mocking him and saying,
     'Come down from that cross and we will believe.'
There are times, Father, when I say to him,
    'Come down from that cross, Jesus,
    so I can have permission to get down from mine.'
In my heart, Lord, I know there was no way
    for him to come down from his cross.
Though he is risen now, there is a sense
    in which he is so attached to that cross
    he will lie on it as long as time lasts.
He is hungry, thirsty, naked, abandoned, crucified,
    wherever any follower of his is
     hungry, thirsty, naked, abandoned, crucified.
I know that if Jesus had come down from his cross
    belief would never have been possible.
He would have proven he was not the Christ
    but only a ghost dressed up in the body of a man.
Now there is no mistaking Jesus is a man like us:
    when soldiers beat him he was bruised;
    when they nailed him to the cross,
     he stayed there and bled.
Since Jesus wanted so much to be like us,
    we too should want to be like him.
If any man will be my disciple, he said,
    let him take up his cross and follow me.
Father, I see in every age and every place
    a cheerful army of quiet people,
    each shouldering a wooden beam
     and following the Carpenter from Galilee.

Humbled and exalted

Father, Jesus frequently said,
 The humble will be exalted.
On the cross he humbled himself in such a way
 that everyone can see he is exalted.
He said,
 'When I am lifted up from the earth,
 I will draw all men to myself.'
Father, I thank you
 that I do not have to avert my eyes from the cross
 to know that Jesus is risen from the dead
 and exalted at your right hand.
Even in death, he is one with you
 and wonderful to us.
He is at once humbled and exalted
 speechless and most eloquent
 fixed to the cross and the freest of men
 dead, and alive with you for ever.
'If you continue in my word,' he said,
 'you are truly my disciples,
 and you will know the truth
 and the truth will make you free.'
Father, help us to continue in Christ's word
 and to be his disciples
 by shouldering our cross
 and following him.
For only in the cross will we find
 truth and freedom.
And only in the cross will we experience for ourselves
 that those who humble themselves
 will be exalted.

Born in a grave

Father, on the night before he died,
Jesus said to his disciples:
  'Truly, truly, I say to you,
  you will weep and lament
    but the world will rejoice;
  you will be sorrowful,
    but your sorrow will turn into joy.
  When a woman is in travail,
    she has sorrow because her hour has come;
  but when she is delivered of the child,
    she no longer remembers the anguish
  for joy that a human being is born into the world.'
Now that Christ has been born again, Father,
  the travail of his followers is over.
For a little while they suffered terribly,
  but when they saw him again,
  their hearts rejoiced with a joy
    no one could take away from them.
Father, give us joy in Christ's delivery from death,
  and 'let us walk cheerfully with him over the earth,
    greeting that of God in every man.'
Even when we are thought fools for Christ's sake,
  or when, through serving him,
    we are cut dead,
let us rejoice on that day
  and leap with joy
as Christ leaped joyfully on to his cross, knowing that,
  for all the humiliation and pain,
    you, Father, were with him always,
  and his reward was very great in heaven.

Waiting

Father, give us patience.
Give us the patience
  you gave to Jesus' disciples
    on Holy Saturday.
It is a time of waiting.
Jesus, we know, had to suffer to become the Christ;
the grain of wheat had to fall
  into the ground and die,
  or else it would have remained for ever alone.
This is why we are waiting, Lord.
We are waiting quietly in the peace of the Spirit.
We are waiting for the harvest to appear.
We are waiting for the night to end.
Jesus is buried in the depths of the tomb
  and has taken our hearts with him.
This is why we say with the Psalmist:
  Out of the depths I cry to you, O Lord,
    Lord, hear my voice.
  Let your ear be attentive
    to the voice of my pleading.
  I am waiting for the Lord
    more than watchman for daybreak,
    more than watchman for daybreak.
Lord, we trust in you.
We place all our hope in your redeeming love.
No night is darker than the tomb's.
But, Father, we believe this buried Seed will spring up,
  the first fruits of the harvest of the dead.
We believe this sunken Sun will rise
  and never set again.

Part IV

CHRIST
THE CONQUEROR
OF DEATH

He is risen

Father, Easter is the festival of light;
  the sun which rose on Easter day will never set.
Easter is the festival of life;
  henceforward death will have no dominion.
As soon as day broke,
  three brave women who watched Jesus die,
  went tearfully to his tomb
    to anoint his body for its burial.
The dawn was only then whitening the eastern sky;
  the Sabbath was barely over.
But already, Father, you had left your Sabbath rest.
You had come down on quiet wings,
  anointing Jesus with the Holy Spirit
    to make him Lord and Christ.
The women were deeply puzzled and perturbed.
How could women
  who have mourned their loved ones since time began
  understand this unprecedented thing :
    the emptying of a grave?
How could they know that Christ the Sun of Justice
  had come forth from death,
    like a bridegroom leaving his room,
  and, like a strong man, run his course with joy?
Today when we awoke, Lord,
  it seemed like any other Spring day.
Crows were nesting in tall trees;
  lambs were gambolling in the fields;
  a slight wind was caressing the faces of the houses.
How were we to know that in the night
  Death had folded up his tent
    and gone away?

The Spring-time of the body

Father, deepen our faith in the resurrection of the dead.
The dead are sown in the earth like seeds.
You, Lord, are the husbandman;
  only you know how you will raise them.
But we believe with Paul that whereas
  what is sown is perishable,
    what is raised is imperishable;
  what is sown in dishonour,
    is raised in glory;
  what is sown in weakness,
    is raised in power;
  what is sown as a body for this world,
    is raised as a body for heaven,
      a body fit for the Lord.
When, Father, with Easter eyes
  we look upon your world,
  we see how the whole of nature,
    for our consolation,
  is meditating on future resurrection.
The sun goes down and comes to birth;
  the stars disappear and return to us;
  the flowers die and come alive again;
  after withering away the vineyards come to leaf;
  nor do seeds, except they die,
    grow green again.
So is the body in the tomb like trees in winter,
  which, under the semblance of aridity,
    conceal the life within.
So it is that we too must await
  the spring-time of the body.[1]

[1] Translated from a prayer by an early Christian, Minucius Felix.

The Sleeper who awoke

Father, your faithful servant Job was grieved
　　that when he went to sleep in death
　　　　no one could ever wake him.
There is hope for a tree, he cried.
Cut it down and it will sprout again;
　　its shoots will not disappear.
Though its roots age in the earth
　　and the stump of it die in the ground,
yet at the water's scent it buds again,
　　putting forth branches like a young plant.
But as for man, he dies and is laid low;
　　he breathes his last, and where is he?
Your servant Paul was inspired with a different belief.
We have our treasure, it is true, in vessels of clay
　　and they crack easily.
But their fragility, Father, is the proof
　　that the fullness of power belongs to you alone.
Paul said, We are afflicted in every way
　　but certainly not crushed.
We are perplexed but not driven to despair,
　　persecuted but not forsaken,
　　stricken but not destroyed.
Where, Lord, did Paul derive such confidence
　　if not from the Man who died on Calvary?
We praise you, Father, because
　　when Jesus went to sleep in death
　　　　you wakened him;
　　when he was laid low like a tree
　　you revived him with the scent of that Water
　　　　which is the Holy Spirit.

Sower and Seed

Father, without the dying of the seed
   there is no harvest.
What you sow, Paul says, does not come to life
   unless it dies.
And what you sow is not the body which is to be
   but a bare kernel of wheat.
Jesus understood the mystery of life and death.
When the hour came for the Son of Man to be glorified,
   he said to his anxious disciples:
Truly, truly, I say to you,
   unless a grain of wheat falls into the earth and dies
     it remains alone;
   but if it dies, it bears much fruit.
Christ knew, Father, that he had to lose his life
   to keep it safe unto eternity.
But he feared like any man to cast himself
   into the deep black furrow of death,
     being both Sower and Seed.
Without the comfort of your Holy Spirit, Father,
   he could not have endured the agony
     and terrible troubling of his soul.
Christ, Seed of Abraham,
   I praise and worship you
   for daring to cast yourself into the ground,
     a bare kernel of wheat.
Father of our Lord Jesus Christ,
   I praise and worship you
   for bringing to life this lonely Seed
   in a lovely harvest, rich and gold,
     more than a hundred-fold.

Christ's Easter Face

Father, at the ceremony of the Easter Vigil,
   we stood for a while in darkness.
Unseeing and unseen, we represented all mankind
   blind from the world's birth.
It was as if chaos and dark night had returned
   and we were waiting for you, God, to say again,
      Let there be light!
Then came Christ, the Light of the World,
   and we knew that never again
      would we have to walk in darkness.
From the orange flame of the Paschal Candle
   the Light spread among us worshippers
      until the old night was gone.
We looked at each other in Christ's glow and saw
   we were children of Light.
We felt that he was among us for ever
   and that his light is the life of men.
We confessed that all the darkness in the world
   would never put out this light.
We confessed that all the evil in the world
   would never put this life to death.
We thank you, Father, for letting us behold
   the light of the gospel of the glory of Christ
      who is the likeness of God.
For it is you, God, who said,
   Let light shine in darkness,
      who shone in our hearts
   to give the light of the knowledge of your glory
      in Christ's Easter Face.

Death without its sting

Father, it takes a brave man to look unflinchingly
  on the face of death.
Such a man was Ecclesiastes, the Preacher.
In common with many people today
  he did not believe in life after death;
but unlike them he did not foolishly shy away from it,
nor 'forget' it until it unmistakably drew near.
All go to one place, he said, both man and beast alike.
All of us are going back to the home from which we came:
  our parent dust.
There is a time for everything under heaven,
  a time for being born and a time to die.
Death's time will come, unplanned and unforeseen,
    when the dust of which we are made returns to the earth
      and our spirit to the God who gave it.
Enjoy life, the Preacher says, obeying God's law,
  but never forget that all is vanity.
Father, I thank you that in Christ you showed us
  there is a fullness of time and a brighter way.
Adam, the first man, was from the earth, a man of dust;
  Christ, the second man, is from heaven.
We bear the image of the man of dust;
  but we bear as well the image of the man of heaven.
We thank you, Father,
  that through Christ's courage on Calvary,
    we too can look unflinchingly on death.
We thank you that after his resurrection we can cry,
  Death is swallowed up in victory.
    O Death, where is thy victory?
    O Death, where is thy sting?
You have given us, God, victory over death
  through our Lord Jesus Christ
    whom you raised from the dead on Easter day.

The Gardener

Father, we believe it is your will for us
   that we should dwell in a Paradise-Garden.
If we do not,
   it is because we are not yet worthy of it.
From the beginning Mankind has disobeyed you, Father,
   and so he cannot reach and eat of the fruit
     of the tree of life.
This is why Christ came:
   to give us life and still more life.
The dead tree of his cross
   has become for us the leafy tree of life
   and the source of all our knowledge and wisdom.
Father, when Mary Magdalen was looking for her Lord,
   she saw him in the Garden close to Calvary
   and you inspired her to think he was the Gardener.
That resurrection-garden is indeed our new Eden,
   our Paradise regained
   wherein Mankind will be creation's Lord
   and which, with Christ, he will tend in peace for ever.
In the heavenly city there will be
   the river of the water of life,
     bright as crystal,
   flowing through the middle of the city's street
     from the throne of God and of the Lamb.
On either side of the river,
   there will stand the tree of life
with its twelve kinds of fruit
   yielding its fruit every month;
and the leaves of the tree
   are for the healing of the nations.

Doubting Thomas

Father, Jesus only became Christ
  by suffering and dying on the cross.
This is why his disciples will always remember him
  with the glorious marks of crucifixion
    upon his risen body.
Thomas, like the rest of the apostles,
  did not believe that God's Anointed
    could end his days on a cross.
He was slower to be convinced than they
  that Jesus was made alive on Easter day.
'Unless I see,' he said, 'the nails' marks in his hands
  and place my fingers in those marks
  and place my hand in his side,
    I will not believe.'
Eight days passed and, though the door was locked,
  the disciples saw their risen Lord
    and, this time, Thomas saw him, too.
Jesus said to Thomas:
  'Trace the marks of my hands with your finger.
  Put your hand into my side.
  And be not faithless but believing.'
Then Thomas saw Jesus crucified was the Christ of God.
  'My Lord and my God,' he cried.
Jesus said: 'Have you believed because you have seen me?
  Blessed are those who have not seen and have believed.'
Father, I am blessed because not with my eyes of flesh
  but with the eye of faith
    I have seen my risen Lord.
And I confess that not even the solid wall of death
  can keep away from us
    him who is Emmanuel,
      God always with us and among us.

The wounds of peace

Father, you are a God of peace,
    and your dearest wish
        is to bless your people with peace.
Jerusalem was of old 'the city of peace',
    symbol of the eternal rest
        you have prepared for your people.
'Rejoice with Jerusalem,' said Isaiah,
    'and be glad for her,
    all you who love her;
that you may drink and be satisfied
    with her consoling breasts;
that you may drink deeply with delight
    from the fullness of her glory.'
Then, Lord, in your name the prophet says:
'As one whom his mother comforts
    so will I comfort you;
    you will be comforted in Jerusalem.'
But Christ who is our peace
    wept over Jerusalem for stoning the prophets
    and not knowing the things that make for peace.
And there, outside the city, he himself was crucified.
But he made peace with you, Father,
    through his blood shed on Calvary.
And when he met his disciples in Jerusalem
    after he was risen,
he said to them Shalom, Peace be with you,
    and showed them his hands and his side.
Christ Jesus, show us your sacred wounds
    so we too may understand
        the meaning of peace.

On the shore of Galilee

Father, give us the grace to accept
  the forgiveness you keep offering us in Christ.
How often we are tempted to despair as Judas did
   when, having betrayed Jesus with a kiss,
    he went and hanged himself.
This is why I marvel at Peter's humility,
  for he, despite his former cowardice and apostasy,
  returned shame-faced to Christ to ask forgiveness.
Before Golgotha, he had boasted aloud,
  'I will die for you but not deny you, Lord,'
and then he denied him three times
  that very night before cock-crow.
Now on the bank of the familiar lake,
  in the light of a new dawn,
three times the risen Christ asked Peter pointedly,
  'Simon, son of John, do you love me?'
And Peter could only tell his Lord
  to look into his heart.
'Yes, Lord,' he whispered, 'you know I love you.'
And Christ said, 'Feed my lambs and feed my sheep.'
Father, I praise you for the strength of Christ
  who can build his Church
   upon the rock of a weak man's faith.
I praise you for the generosity of Christ
  who chose as his chief shepherd
  someone who deserted him
   in his hour of need.
Father, help me to be humble when I fail,
  and in all I do to let Christ take my arm
   and lead me wheresoever he wills.

Emmaus and the broken bread

Father, it is strange how often
  the dearest things seem unfamiliar
  the nearest things seem very far away.
On Easter day, Jesus was not recognized
  when he walked with two of his disciples to Emmaus.
He spoke to them and listened to them;
  and proved to them how necessary it was
  for the Christ to suffer if he was to enter his glory.
He made them see as well that Calvary
  was all of a piece with Moses and the prophets.
Inspired by his presence, the disciples pleaded with him,
  'Stay with us, for night is coming on
    and the day is almost spent.'
Christ incognito agreed and sat down with them at table.
He assumed the role of host:
  he took the bread, blessed it, broke it
    and gave them both a share of it.
It was through this everyday action that they knew him;
  and immediately he vanished from their sight.
Father, once more Christ delivers himself
  into his disciples' hands.
In the simple gesture of the breaking of the bread
  he gives himself away;
and though we do not see him any more,
  we believe he is always in our midst.
His Holy Spirit is a burning presence in our hearts;
  and in our hands is broken and divided Bread.
Father, give us this food
  that will sustain us on life's journey
  and save us from being frightened
    by the long and lonely night.

The Man who empties graves

Father, when Israel was in Exile, the Psalmist wrote:
  'By the waters of Babylon,
      there we sat and wept
  when we remembered Zion.'
Israel grieved for her exiles as for the dead.
This is why Ezekiel saw in a vision
  a valley of bones which were very dry.
The Lord God said to him,
  'Son of man can these bones live?'
  and he replied, 'Lord, only you know that.'
The Lord said again: 'Prophesy to these bones
  and say, Dry bones, hear the word of the Lord.'
There was a swelling noise and lo, a rattling;
  and all the bones came together
      and flesh covered them;
  but there was no breath in them.
Then the Lord told Ezekiel to summon the breath:
  'Come from the four winds, O breath,
  and breathe upon these slain, that they may live.'
The prophet summoned the breath;
  and from the bones a whole host came alive.
These bones were Israel, hopeless, dried up, dead.
'But,' said the Lord God,
  'Behold, I will open your graves
      and raise you from your graves, O my people.
  And I will put my Spirit within you and you will live,
      for I will place you in your own land.'
Father, I thank you that in Christ the hour has come
  when our long exile in the land of Death is over.
The Son of Man has summoned up the breath of your Spirit;
  and all of us in Death's grave have heard his voice,
      and we shall live.

Communion with the departed

Father, Christ is the first fruits
  of those who have fallen asleep.
When the women went to Jesus' tomb,
  hoping to anoint his body for burial,
two mysterious figures in dazzling white enquired of them,
  'Why are you seeking the living among the dead?'
I thank you, Father, that you did not let
  your Holy One see corruption,
  but soon awakened him from his sleep of death.
And this is why we do not grieve
  for our loved ones who have fallen asleep
  as others do who have no hope.
This at least we know: Christ died for us,
  so that whether we wake or sleep
    we are always with the Lord.
Father, we believe Christ when he said,
  'The hour is coming, it has come already,
    when the dead will hear the voice of God's Son
    and those who hear it will live.
For as the Father has life in himself,
    so has he given this life to his Son.
The hour is coming when all who are in the tomb
    will hear his voice and come forth,
  those who have done well
    to the resurrection of life,
  those who have done ill
    to the resurrection of judgement.
Father, help us grieve no more for our dear ones
  who have fallen asleep
but commit them trustingly
  to Christ the Conqueror of Death.

The Ascension

Father, on Ascension day the Easter candle is extinguished,
   and in the smoke ascending from the wick
      we see an image of Christ's heavenly ascension.
At the Passover feast, Jesus already knew
   his hour had come for him to pass over
      from this world unto you.
'Father,' he said, 'I have glorified you on the earth;
   I have finished the work you gave me to do.
   Now, Father, glorify me in your presence
      with the glory which I had with you
      before the world began.'
Father, you glorified Jesus on his cross;
   and on this day he ascends to you
      to enter his glory everlastingly.
He is our High Priest who has passed through the heavens.
He has entered the true sanctuary on high
   where he offers up for us unceasingly
      the once-for-all sacrifice of his life.
Because of him, Father, we too
   have access to the heavenly sanctuary through his blood.
The curtain of this sanctuary was his flesh;
   and his flesh was rent asunder on the cross
      so that we might go through it to you, God,
      and meet you with confidence and a pure heart.
Through hope our hearts are anchored in the heavens;
   and we feel already something of your Sabbath rest.
Father, today Christ is seated at your right hand.
Lift our minds above the earth to heavenly things.
For in a sense we, too, have died,
   and our life is hidden away with Christ in God.

A High Priest, merciful and faithful

Father, we thank you for sending your Son into the world
    to be one with us in all our sorrows and joys.
He was a man no different from ourselves.
We are flesh and blood and so was he.
Our nature was in the powerful grip of death
    and yet he willingly took this nature to himself
    so that in himself he could conquer death
      and become the life of the world.
In every respect, Father, he became like us
    so that we could turn to him,
      our High Priest, merciful and faithful,
    and know that since he suffered and was tempted
      he could comfort us in all our trials.
Father, we thank you that we do not have a High Priest
    who is unable to sympathize with our weaknesses.
For Christ was tempted in every way as we are,
    though he did not sin.
This is why he can be so gentle
    with all the foolish and the wayward,
      for he himself is vulnerable in every way.
And so, Father, we need never come to you alone.
Of ourselves, we have nothing that could win your favour.
This is why we come in company with your beloved Son,
    knowing that you always hear his prayer
      which he never ceases offering up for us.
With him, we draw near with confidence
    to the throne of grace,
believing that because of Christ, our High Priest,
    we will obtain mercy and find grace
      whenever we need it.

The last blessing

Father, you are the blessed God
    because you are the only source
        of life and holiness.
At the origins of our race,
    you blessed mankind, saying,
    'Be fruitful, multiply and fill the earth
        and be the lord of it.'
And you have never ceased to bless us, Father,
    even though we frequently refuse your gifts.
If we bless you, Father, in return
    it is because we are conscious of your kindness to us
        and of all the marvels you have done for us.
When the time came for Jesus to return to you,
    he led his disciples out to Bethany;
    and then he lifted up his hands
        and blessed them solemnly.
It was while he was blessing them
    that he parted from them
        and went to you, his Father.
This is how we, his followers, still remember him:
    his nail-torn hands are raised
        in an eternal benediction.
When the disciples returned to Jerusalem that day
    they joyfully chanted blessings to you, God.
For they knew that Jesus who had been crucified
    would never lower his wounded Christed hands;
and from them would come soon
    your best and most enduring blessing:
        the gift of the Holy Spirit.

Part V

CHRIST SENDS
HIS SPIRIT

Waiting for the Father's Promise

Father, waiting can be the hardest part of life.
Children cannot wait to see the seeds they've sown
    turn into flowers.
Many youngsters cannot wait to get married.
Many old people cannot wait to die.
Just before Jesus ascended to his Father,
    he told his disciples to stay in Jerusalem
      and wait there for the Promise of the Father
        which was their baptism in the Holy Spirit.
Father, it is hardest of all to wait for you
    when we desperately need your Strength and Comfort
      to face the many trials of life.
This is why the Psalmist says repeatedly
    we must be still before the Lord
      and wait patiently for him;
    we must quieten our soul
      and wait for the Lord in prayerful silence.
Sometimes we feel, Father,
    that you have forgotten us
    that you wander like a stranger through our land.
Then we remember you are the everlasting God,
    Creator of the earth and all it contains.
When youths and young men fall exhausted,
    you give the weak and old your strength
    so they rise as though on eagles' wings.
Teach me, Father, to be like Christ's disciples
    as they wait for the coming of the Spirit.
Teach me always to wait quietly for you
    and to possess my soul in patience.

The Wind and the Fire

Father, Pentecost is the festival of light.
Today the sun which dawned on Easter morning
   has climbed to the meridian
      and will not wane or set.
Today a new world has begun
   when the Spirit of perpetual Spring
      who joined you and your Christ
in an eternal fond embrace of love
   has united men of every nation under heaven
      in a single family.
Today the Spirit comes in Wind and Fire
   upon the City of Peace;
and from Jerusalem this peace is spreading wildly
   to Judea, Samaria,
      and thence to the ends of the earth.
Father, let me feel something of
   the warm hurricane of love
      that strikes Jerusalem
so that I, too, through a Spirit-filled life,
   may be a witness of the peace of Christ.
And may you, great Pentecostal Spirit,
   never cease coming to our hearts
to excite, illuminate and warm them.
   Holy Spirit, come we pray,
   And a single heavenly ray
      Of thy Light to us impart.
   Come thou Father of the poor,
   Come thou Gift which will endure,
      Come thou Brightness of the heart.

The Comforter has come

Father, at the Supper,
   Jesus uttered these mysterious words:
      'It is better for you I should go away,
      for if I do not go away,
      the Comforter will not come to you,
      but if I go, I will send him to you.'
Jesus had to die to become the Christ;
   he had to empty himself to be filled with the Spirit.
But, Father, we know that the Spirit
   is not our comfort in Christ's absence
   but the One who guarantees his constant presence.
Jesus said: 'I will not leave you desolate;
   I will come to you.'
He comes in the comforting of his Spirit.
Happy, then, are we, Father, who mourn Jesus' death,
   for we are comforted with Christ's Spirit.
Father of mercies and God of all comfort,
   send the Comforter on us
   especially in times of sorrow and bereavement.
Through his comforting presence
   may we always find communion in Christ
      with those we love, whether we live or die.
Holy Spirit, we pray for your warmth and your consolation.
   Of Consolers thou art best,
   In our hearts the dearest Guest,
      Dearest Friend through all the years.
   After work our rest at night,
   Shade against the sun's fierce light,
      Solace when we are in tears.

The shining of the Spirit

Father, you are Light
and in you there is no darkness at all.
You alone have immortality
and dwell in light so unapproachable
no man has ever seen you or can see you.
But in Christ, Father,
you lifted up the light of your countenance on us.
He is the Light of the world,
for he reflects the glory of your face,
the glory which is your Holy Spirit.
In heaven the night is ended.
There is no need of lamp or sun or moon
because the Lamb is the lamp of the city
and your glory is its light.
And even here, Father, we are seeing this light
which comes into the world in Christ.
Death seemed to extinguish the light;
but your Spirit rekindled the Lamp
and it will shine for ever more.
Spirit of the risen Christ,
shine brightly on us
so we may walk as children of light
and have our long lost innocence restored to us.
Of all lights thou loveliest Light,
Shine on us and chase the night
From the crannies of our soul.
Nothing is more certain than
Without thee there is in man
Nothing innocent or whole.

God's greatest Gift

Father, we thank you for your greatest Gift:
   the Holy Spirit,
   the love in which you and Christ are one.
The Spirit is the Forgiveness of sins.
Give us this Gift, Father, so that
   though our sins are like scarlet,
     they shall be white as snow;
   though they are red like crimson,
     they shall become white as wool.
Give us this Gift so that
   our parched hearts may become
     like a well-watered garden.
Give us this Gift so that
   our many wounds may heal
   our bigotry may soon relax and bend
   our tepidity may turn to fire
   our errant hearts may cease their wanderings.
We know that every good and perfect gift
   comes down from you, the Father of lights,
   in whom there is no variation,
     no slightest shadow of change.
Give us the perfect Gift of your Holy Spirit
so that in our hearts we may cry out to him:
   Cleanse us of each sinful stain,
   Soak our dryness with thy rain,
     Soothe and heal what suffers pain.
   Unbend fast the bigot's brain,
   Fan all fires that start to wane,
     Bring the lost sheep home again.

The Spirit of joy

Father, in giving us Christ's Spirit,
  you are giving us yourself;
and in giving us yourself,
  you fill our hearts with a joy
    which the world cannot give.
Christ said : If any man thirst,
  let him come to me;
  and let the man drink who believes in me.
  For from my heart shall flow
    rivers of living water.
Out of Christ's heart, pierced on the cross,
  has flown the river of life
    which is your Holy Spirit.
This is why, Father, we go to Christ
  and with joy drink water
    from the deep well of our Saviour.
Father, fill us with joy in believing;
  for what is your kingdom
  if not joy in the Holy Spirit
    now and for ever?
Spirit of our risen Lord,
  give us your many fruits and graces
    especially love and peace and joy.
Breathe into us the breath of your inspiration.
  Grant thy seven-fold Gift to those
  In whose heart thy mercy flows,
    Those with faith and trust in thee.
  Grant them virtue's rich reward,
  Grant them death in Christ their Lord,
    Grant them joy eternally.

Christ pours out his Spirit

Father, I like the abundance implied
  in the English verb 'to pour'.
I am impressed when rain pours down,
  when wine is poured out,
    even when insults are poured on someone's head.
The Psalmist exults when someone worships you, God,
  by pouring out his heart and soul.
Isaiah honours your Suffering Servant
  because he poured out his soul to death.
Father, there was nothing mean or niggardly about Christ.
He was a Man who poured himself away
  for all his brethren.
He emptied himself so you could fill him
  with the best wine of your Spirit.
How could such a magnanimous man
  dispense that Spirit like a shower of rain?
No, Father, having received from you
  the promise of the Holy Spirit,
    he poured it out on all flesh.
No wonder that from the day of Pentecost
  young men see visions
  and old men dream dreams.
Lord Jesus, pour out your Spirit on me
  like rain from an open sky
  like water cascading down a mountain-side.
For only then will Isaiah's dream come true:
  my soul's desert will become a fruitful field;
  and the fruitful field shall seem
    rich as a forest full of tall clean pines.

The Spirit of peace

Father, at the Supper, Jesus said:
  Peace I leave with you;
  my peace I give to you;
  not as the world gives do I give to you.
The peace Christ left with us, Father,
  is the peace of the Dove,
    the gentle presence of the Holy Spirit.
In Christ you blessed your people with peace,
  because in him we find the Spirit
    of love and reconciliation.
Over the troubled waters of his disciples' hearts,
  the risen Christ said, 'Peace, be still!'
and the winds fell and the waves ceased
  and at last they found themselves to be men of peace.
Whatever tribulations they had in the world,
  in Christ they had peace,
    for he had overcome the world.
The risen Christ breathed on them;
  and borne upon his breath
    was the Dove of your divine forgiveness;
and they blessed you, Father, for your grace and peace.
Father, may the Whitsuntide Christ
  breathe his Spirit of peace on me.
Make me worthy to be called your child
  by making me an instrument of your peace.
In the Holy Spirit, Father,
  I have calmed and quieted my soul
    like a child quieted at its mother's breast;
  like a child that is quieted is my soul.

The Spirit and the birth

Father, today I walk before you like a child.
I would not now dare speak with you as my Father
   had not Christ himself persuaded me.
He first with infinite daring called you 'Father';
   and now that word, that fond and frightening word,
     is on my lips as I come to you
   through Christ, with Christ, in Christ.
Whenever we cry Abba! Father!
   it is Christ's Spirit praying inside us,
   witnessing together with our spirit
     that we are your children.
And if, Father, we are your children,
   are we not your heirs as well,
     co-heirs with Christ? —
   provided we behave as your children should.
I open my eyes, Father, and seem to see
   the whole world groaning like a mother
     in childbirth-agony.
What is to be the issue of it
   but your children, God?
Our high vocation means
   that birth in the Spirit
     will sometimes feel like death.
We, too, who have within us the first fruits of the Spirit
   groan inwardly as we await
     our adoption as sons, the redemption of our bodies.
Father, while we wait,
   not knowing how to pray as we ought,
   the Spirit within assists us in our weakness.
Thank you for sending the Spirit of your Son
   to intercede for us with sighs
     too deep for
       words.

Praying in the Spirit

Father, when I am not understood,
    I tend to say I have not been listened to.
But, to speak honestly, I ought not to be surprised.
Within me, besides thoughts and feelings,
    are whisperings and shadows.
My spirit perceives them;
    but I am not able to share them with others.
My spirit longs to say to people:
    This is what I think and feel;
    this is what I'm trying to do.
But I cannot find the right word.
They would have to be me to understand.
But when I turn to you, Father,
    I find with joy I am completely understood.
In my prayer, without speaking,
    I always find the right Word.
Between you and me, there is this quiet,
    this effortless communion in Christ my Lord.
For you have given me Christ's Spirit
    who comprehends your thoughts;
and the Spirit sighs within me
    at a level far too deep for words.
It is the Spirit who assures me that,
    although I cannot begin to express myself,
    you know me through and through
    and I know you in your creative Word.
Father, I thank you that the Spirit who made
    Christ's birth possible
    his life fruitful
    his death victorious
has been given to me so that
    my heart may speak directly to your heart.

A Fountain of Water

Father, you contain within yourself the waters of life,
  and everyone who thirsts
    must come to you to drink.
The Psalmist wrote passionately:
  'As the deer longs for running streams,
    so my soul is longing for you, my God.
  My soul is thirsting for God, the living God.
    When will I be allowed to see the face of God?'
Again he says with equal ardour:
  'O God, you are my God, I long for you;
    my soul is thirsting for you.
  My body is panting for you,
    as in a dry, weary land without water.'
Father, alas, such longings I seldom experience.
I am rather to be numbered among your people
  who have perpetrated two wrongs:
we have forsaken you, the fountain of living waters,
  and dug for ourselves cisterns,
    leaky cisterns that can hold no water.
On a hot midday at the well of Samaria,
  Jesus said to the woman drawing from the well:
  'Everyone who drinks of this water will thirst again,
  but whoever drinks of the water I will give
    will never thirst.
  The water I will give will become in him
    a fountain of water bubbling up to eternal life.'
Father, I have seen this water
  streaming from the pierced heart of Jesus crucified.
Give me a drink of this precious water of the Spirit
  so I may never thirst again.

Father, Son and Holy Spirit

Father, when Philip said to Jesus,
　'Lord, show us the Father
　　and it will be enough for us,'
Jesus replied, 'Have I been so long with you,
　and still you do not know me, Philip?
Whoever has seen me has seen the Father, too;
　so how can you say, "Show us the Father"?
Do you not believe that I am in the Father,
　and the Father is in me?'
Father, I confess you are the everlasting God
　whom no one has ever seen or can see.
But I believe that in Christ your Word
　you have shown yourself to be our Father
　and poured out your Spirit on all mankind.
In that timeless beginning from which sprang
　the world's beginning,
you lived with your Spirit and your Word in love.
And yet Christ's followers all dare to speak of
　that which was from the beginning,
　which we have heard, which we have seen with our eyes,
　which we have gazed upon and handled
　　concerning the Word of life.
For the life was disclosed to us
　and we saw it and witness to it
　　and cry aloud to others
　the eternal life which was with you, Father,
　　and was disclosed to us.
We thank you, hidden God,
　for disclosing yourself in Christ
　　as our provident and gentle Father,
and for bringing us into the beautiful fellowship
　of your Holy Spirit.

Part VI

THE WONDER OF
LIFE IN CHRIST

The miracle of birth

Father, I thank you for the immense surprise
    of letting me be born.
Fifty years ago I was nothing.
Fifty years hence I will be nothing.
It seems wonderful to me and strange that on this earth
    I once did not exist, need not, will not;
        but *do* exist.
If I were a stone, a bird, a blade of grass,
    it would be good to be in existence for an hour,
        under your wise and gentle providence.
But you have breathed into my heart
    your own Breath,
        the everlasting Spirit;
and in my mind is the prospect of eternal things.
When I look at the heavens, the work of your hands,
    the moon and the stars which you arranged,
what is man that you keep him in mind,
    the son of man that you care for him?
Yet you have made him little less than a god;
    with glory and honour you crowned him.
You have made him lord over the works of your hands
    and put all things under his feet.
Father, I come before you in Christ,
    asking you to flood my soul with wonder
        at the gracious gift of life.
My prayer is: may no day pass
    but I praise you for your goodness
        in creating me.
O Lord, our Lord,
    how majestic is your name in all the earth!

Made new each morning

Father, it is a commonplace
  that as soon as we start to live
    we start to die.
Even for the oldest of us life is brief;
  and in its beginning and its end
    we experience the extremes of human frailty.
The infirmities of age distress and humble us.
We watch the old
  dragging themselves along like grasshoppers.
Their hair is white
  like blossom on the almond tree.
They do not hear too well
  or see too well
  or sleep too well.
And we shudder, knowing that what time has done to them,
  it will one day do to us.
Paul looked upon old age quite differently.
'We do not lose heart,' he wrote.
'Though our outer self is wasting away,
  our inner self is being renewed day by day.
You cannot compare our troubles,
  light and not long-lasting,
    with the eternal glory they are gaining us.
For we do not look to things that are seen
  but to things that are unseen.
The things that are seen are passing,
  whereas things unseen are everlasting.'
Father, we ask you to brighten our vision
  so that we may rejoice in all the phases of life;
for we know that even when we are sick and old
  you make us new again each morning.

God chooses strangely

Father, whenever we think of ourselves
   as the followers of Christ,
   we smile a Sarah-like smile of incredulity.
Poor Jesus, to have us for his disciples!
   What can we do for him?
   How can we further his cause?
We are such ordinary people
   with very little energy or learning
   and precious few talents to boast of.
Our one grain of comfort is that from the beginning,
   when Christ called his apostles
     after a night of prayer,
he did not pick people who were wise
   by any worldly standards;
he did not pick people who were powerful
   or of noble birth.
We are encouraged by the fact that you chose
   the foolish to make fools of the wise,
   the weak to make fools of the strong.
God, we thank you for choosing the little people
   and the lowly people,
   for choosing what is really nothing at all
so as to bring to nothing the wise, the great, the strong.
Why, Lord, have you acted in so strange a way?
It is so that no human being
   could possibly boast before you.
You, Father, are the source of all the treasures
   we find hidden in Christ Jesus.
You made him who was crucified in weakness
   into our wisdom, holiness and strength,
     and our release from sin.
Now, Lord, if we boast, we will only boast in you.

When I am weak

Father, deepen my conviction that
    when I am weak, then I am strong.
Too often I rely on my own gifts and capacities
    when I should rely entirely on you.
I believe your strength is most plainly revealed
    in the cross of Jesus Christ.
The cross is both weakness and folly
    to those who trust in worldliness.
But how can I doubt, Lord, that in Christ crucified
    is your power to heal and save us?
This is why scripture says:
    'I will lay in ruins the wisdom of the wise.
    The cleverness of the clever I will thwart.'
With Paul, I desire to know nothing, Father,
    except Jesus Christ and him crucified.
What is required of us is that we should show others
    in our living and dying
        the love shown us by Jesus crucified.
It is difficult at first to stop relying
    on our own talents and achievements.
But, in the end, Lord, there is only peace and joy
    in knowing we cannot save ourselves,
    but only deliver ourselves into your hands.
        our Father and our God.
Help me, then, to trust in you
    and to boast of nothing
        but the cross of our Lord Jesus Christ,
by which the world is nailed to me
    and I am nailed to the world.

If I must boast

Father, it is not our strength that commends us to you
  but our weakness and humility.
You are a God who exalts the humble
  and humbles the exalted.
Paul was a disciple who could have boasted
  if he had had a mind to boast.
Had he not planted the Church of Christ in many lands?
For Christ's sake he had endured
  beatings and imprisonment
  stonings and shipwreck.
He had been in peril from rivers and robbers,
  from Jews and Gentiles.
He had faced danger in cities and deserts,
  dangers at sea and on the land.
No apostle had suffered more than he
  from cold and heat, hunger and thirst,
    anxiety and sleeplessness.
He had been let down the wall of Damascus in a basket
  and felt disgraced by that.
But he had also been lifted up into Paradise
  so he could not tell
    whether he was in his body or out of it.
After all this, what does he boast of?
  Only of his weakness.
  Only of the fierce thorn in his flesh
    that stopped him being proud and puffed up.
He knew, Father, that your grace was enough for him
  and your power was perfected in his weakness.
With Paul I gladly boast of my weakness
  so that Christ's power may rest on me
    and his Spirit may strengthen me.

Making impossible things possible

Father, I thank you for the generosity
  of our Lord Jesus Christ,
who, though he was infinitely rich,
  became a pauper for our sakes
    to enrich us with his poverty.
Jesus knew the happiness of the poor.
He was a cheerful giver;
  and gave away everything he had to the poor.
When he died, his hands were empty
  save for the nails.
Father, like the apostles, I am frightened
  by Jesus' teaching on possessions.
'It is easier,' he said,
  'to thread a camel through a needle's eye,
  than for a rich man to enter God's kingdom.'
The disciples asked,
  'How, then, can anyone be saved?'
He answered,
  'It is not possible for men;
  but God makes impossible things possible.'
Father, among the many perils of the rich are
  insensitivity towards the miseries of the poor;
  reliance on self instead of reliance on you;
  a harshness of soul that comes from having
    every wish and whim immediately fulfilled.
Father, do the impossible thing: make me rich towards you.
Let me not say,
  'I am rich, I have prospered, I need nothing,'
when really I am wretched and pitiable,
  poor and blind and naked.

The Bread of Life

Father, you have given us Jesus Christ
    who is the true bread from heaven.
He is the manna of the new covenant
    which came down from heaven
        and gives life to the world.
Jesus said,
    'I am the bread of life;
    he who comes to me will not hunger,
        and he who believes in me will never thirst.'
Father, deepen my faith in Christ
    so he may fill me with eternal life
        and raise me up at the last day.
Feed me with Christ's own body and blood,
    for unless I eat his flesh and drink his blood
        I will not have life in me.
For his flesh is real food
    and his blood is real drink,
and when I eat his flesh and drink his blood,
    I abide in him and he abides in me.
Father, let me live by Christ your Son
    as he lives by you;
and then the Spirit of holiness
    by whom you raised Jesus from the dead
    will dwell in me as in his temple;
and he will raise me from the dead at judgement day.
Father, I thank you for inviting me to eat at your table,
    so enabling me to taste for myself
        that the Lord is very sweet.

Lazarus is alive again

Father, though Jesus, like any man, was afraid to die,
  he faced death without flinching
    because he put his trust in you.
'There are but twelve hours in the day,' he said.
  'If anyone walks in the day,
    he does not stumble
  because he sees the light of the world.'
Jesus did not stumble, Father,
  nor did he walk in the night,
    for he was Light itself and Life.
When Martha said to Jesus,
  'Lord, if only you had been here,
  my brother would not have died,'
he answered her,
  'Your brother will rise again.'
Martha said,
  'I know he will rise again
  in the resurrection at the last day.'
Jesus replied :
  'I am the Resurrection and the Life.
  He who believes in me, though he is dead,
    yet shall he live.
  And whoever lives and believes in me,
    shall never die.'
Father, I believe your Christ is Light inextinguishable
  and Life unquenchable.
How can I thank you enough
  for the miracle of letting me hear his voice
    and see the light of his face?
For I was dead and buried, Father,
  and my name is Lazarus.

Mary, Virgin and Mother

Father, I thank you for what you have revealed of yourself
   in Mary's virgin-motherhood.
She was humble so you exalted her;
she was poor so you enriched her;
she was empty so you filled her;
she was your servant so you cared for her;
she had no future, by reason of her virginity,
   so you brought to birth in her
      the world's future, Jesus Christ our Lord.
Mary responded to your message
   with faith and love.
Behold, she said, the slave of the Lord.
   Let the Lord's Word be fulfilled in me.
Lord, through Mary's faith and love and humble service,
   your Word was made flesh
      and dwelt among us.
You exalted Mary your slave
   who humbled herself in her virginity
as you were to exalt your slave Jesus
   when he humbled himself
      even to the death of the cross.
Father, I pray that through the Virgin Mary
   I may learn what you expect of me.
May I become, through grace, humble and poor,
   empty and a slave,
so that you may exalt and enrich me,
so that you may fill me with heavenly blessings
   and bring Christ to birth
      through faith in my heart.

Christ and the widow's mite

Father, make me more spontaneously generous.
The gospels are filled with many striking tales
   of this kind of magnanimity.
When Christ called Peter and Andrew, James and John,
   they immediately left everything to follow him.
He called Matthew, a tax-collector,
   and immediately he closed shop and followed him.
But of all the gospels' tales of generosity
   I am challenged most by the one about a poor widow.
Jesus had been sitting opposite the temple treasury.
He had watched many rich people, as they filed by,
   putting in considerable sums.
Then along came this poor widow.
She put in a couple of copper coins, a mere penny.
Jesus was so excited by this he called his disciples:
'Listen carefully,' he said.
'This poor widow has put in the treasury more than anyone.
The rest gave out of their abundance.
She, out of her poverty, gave everything she had.'
I have often wondered, Father,
   whether that widow was wise in parting with her money,
Her action seems to have been proud and improvident,
   leaving her a penniless nuisance
      and dependent on charity.
But Jesus generously praised her generosity.
Was it, Father, because she was a kindred soul to him
   who was improvident enough to give his all on the cross,
even though it seemed small enough at the time,
   and hardly likely to make
      any difference to the world?

Branches of the Vine

Father, I believe that Christ is the true Vine
  and you are the Vine-dresser.
As for me, I am a branch of Christ.
If I bear no fruit, Father,
  what choice have you but to lop me off?
I pray that I may bear some fruit
  because then you will prune me
    so I can bear more fruit.
Already you have made us healthy
  with the sharp knife of Christ's Word.
And now, Father, we pray we may abide in him
  and he may abide in us.
Branches cannot bear fruit
  unless they live in the vine;
neither can we bear fruit
  unless we abide in him.
He is the Vine and we are his branches.
When we live in him and he lives in us
  we bring forth fruit together.
As we cannot do anything without him,
  neither can he do anything in the world
    without us.
Vine and branches need each other.
We ask you, Father, that we may continue living in Christ
  so you will not have to lop us off
    like dead branches.
Such branches must wither
  and you will have to gather them, careful Father,
and throw them into the fire
  to be burned.

Joy even in affliction

Father, you know how often we are afflicted.
From toothache we suffer and earache
   and, worst of all, from heartache.
This bewilders us for you are infinitely good and strong.
   Why, then, should we have to endure so much?
   Why should the upright have to endure so much?
   Why should little children have to suffer at all?
Jesus, your Son, was wholly innocent
   and still he suffered on the cross.
Was he not right, Lord, to cry out to you,
   'My God, my God, why have you abandoned me?'
Yet, we believe, Father, he did not despair.
   He loved you and us right to the end,
   and at the last, committed his spirit into your keeping.
Lord, we cannot understand your ways;
   your ways are so much higher than our ways.
With Christ, we commit our spirit into your hands,
   strong hands that made the world
     and can remake our lives
   when pain or loss or disappointment
     seem to have shattered them.
And we can do this not merely grudgingly but joyfully.
Teach us, Father, to rejoice
   not *at* our suffering but *in* our suffering.
For we know that suffering produces perseverance
   and perseverance produces character
   and character produces hope
and hope will never be disappointed
   because the Holy Spirit,
     the everlasting Love that fills your heart,
       has been poured into our hearts, too.

A prayer of thanks

Father, my soul and my flesh have thirsted for you,
  and your Son has given to me
   his body for food, his blood for drink,
   his Spirit as a fountain of water within me
    springing up into eternal life.
Made one with Jesus in the Eucharist,
  flesh of his flesh, bone of his bone,
I do not come to you alone, Father, but in your Christ.
He is our wisdom and peace;
  he is our reconciliation with you.
This is why I come to you as one limb
  of that body of which Christ is the head.
It is no longer I who live
  but Christ who lives in me;
and the life I now live in the flesh
  I live by faith in the Son of God
   who loved me and gave himself to me.
Father, we were all dead,
  and you revivified us by your Spirit.
We were broken and soiled,
  but you mended us and washed us.
Father of mercies and God of all comfort,
  you have comforted us with the heavenly manna,
   the body and blood of your Son.
Help us to remain faithful to you in the desert of life;
  and when the exile is over,
   when there is no mourning any more,
    nor sorrow nor weeping,
grant that we may see you then
  not as now in the dark mirror of faith,
   but face to face for ever.

A hope beyond this life

Father, we do not hold with Ecclesiastes
   that the dust is our eternal home.
We believe in the resurrection of the dead
   and life everlasting.
If there is no resurrection of the dead,
   then Christ has not been raised.
If Christ has not been raised,
   then our preaching and our faith
      are all in vain;
   and those who have gone to sleep in Christ
      will lie for ever in the dust.
Father, if in this life only we have hope in Christ,
   we are the most pitiable of men.
But we believe you raised Christ from the dead,
   the first fruits of those who have fallen asleep.
We recognize that for us, too, Father,
   the mourners will one day go about the streets;
   the silver cord that holds
      life's golden lamp will snap;
   the pitcher, once full of water winking in the sun,
      will lie broken at the well.
But we believe, Father, you are the God of the living
   not the dead.
And by your Spirit you have already given us
   communion with the living Christ.
Christ's love has overpowered us,
   convincing us he renounced everything for our sakes.
Grant, Father, that we who live
   may live no longer for ourselves
   but for him who died for us
      and whom you raised from the dead.

Life hereafter

Father, our minds were not made to think about Hereafter.
We have to resort to images and pictures,
   knowing that the reality surpasses them
as love surpasses the stumbling words
   that lovers use.
The Apocalyptist depicts
   a new heaven and a new earth;
for the first heaven and earth had passed away,
   and the sea is no more.
The sea that here has swallowed ships and men
   in the Hereafter will vanish,
     having yielded up its dead.
Then Death and Hades, where the dead dwell,
   will be thrown into the lake of fire
     and die themselves.
Lastly, there will descend from heaven from God
   the holy city, the New Jerusalem,
     made ready as a bride
       adorned for her husband.
Father, through these images we dimly apprehend
   that death will not have final victory
     over those who love you;
and you will dwell with us as a husband dwells
   with his beloved bride, all beautiful.
We thank you, Father, for your promise that
   you will wipe away every tear from our eyes,
and death shall be no more,
   neither mourning nor crying nor pain any more,
because all the former things will have passed away.

Part VII

THE DISCIPLINE OF CHRIST

Remember Man . . .

Father, today we remember that we are dust
  and unto dust we shall return.
Of itself the ash upon our forehead
  should not frighten us.
It is when we lose spiritual integrity
  that bodily disintegration
    acquires a new and threatening meaning.
For when we sin,
  we fall away from you, Father,
    who are eternal life
and become only what we are made of:
  dust.
If we should so die, Father,
  will not the risen Christ be forced
    to shake us off his feet
as he leaves our earthly city for the New Jerusalem?
We pray that in the Lenten days ahead
  we may repent of our sins.
Give us a thorough change of heart
so we may rid our lives
  of wrong-doing and mediocrity,
so we may become holy and Easter-whole again.
Father, our lives are light as dust
  lifted by a summer's wind.
We beg you to send upon us
  the power and comfort of your Spirit
so that Death
  may not daunt us or destroy us utterly
but be our means of passing over with Christ
  from this dark world to everlasting Light.

The fasting chosen by God

Father, help me to be faithful in fasting
   so that in Christ I may draw nearer
      to you and all my brethren.
I know the fast you choose for me
   is not for a single day
      to make a show of my humility.
It is not to bow my head sulkily like a reed
   or wear a long, lugubrious face
   or walk about in solemn Sunday clothes.
The fast you choose for me is to untie
   the rope I've put around my neck,
   the ropes I've put around other people's necks.
The fast you choose for me is
   to share my bread with the hungry
   to bring the homeless home with me
   to give away my clothing to the naked
   to comfort anyone who is lonely or afraid.
I pray, Father, that when this fast is over,
   I may not be prouder than when it began.
Help me so to pour myself out for the hungry
   and to run to the help of those in need,
that light shall break over me like the dawn
   and your healing hand touch me miraculously.
Then, Father, when Easter comes,
   you will reverse the days of fasting,
   satisfying my soul with genuine joy,
   making my spirit feel
      like a watered garden,
      like a flowing spring
         whose waters never fail.

Sincerity in religion

Father, help me during these days of discipline
   to make my religion more sincere.
Too often when I pray, you are forced
   to turn your head away from me
      in embarrassment
because I call you 'Father'
   while not treating my fellows
      as my brothers and sisters.
I go upon my knees in prayer
   but seldom is my spirit humbled
      before God or men.
I worship you
   but do not cease from evil
   or learn to do good.
I go to church
   but do not strive after justice,
   nor am I kind to the unhappy
      or generous to the unfortunate.
With a pious granite face,
   I walk on the other side of every road,
   past countless wounded strangers,
      while I pray hard for the needy.
I am in grave danger, Lord,
   of being lost in my prayers eternally.
Send upon me, Father, Christ's Spirit of sincerity
   lest I become
      like an oak whose leaf is withered
      like an unwatered garden without flowers
      like a spark swallowed up by eternal night.

The discipline of love

Father, I know I cannot serve you well
    without the discipline of love.
Help me to pray
    so that prayer becomes as necessary to me as food.
Help me to fast
    so that I become more alive and sensitive
        to spiritual realities.
Help me to give generously in alms
    so as to be more of a neighbour to a world in need
    and by renouncing a little of the power I have
        over my own life
    to symbolize my dependence on you.
Help me, Father, to discipline myself cheerfully.
    In a race, though all compete,
        only the fastest and the fittest wins.
    A boxer must give up many things
        if he is to win a fight;
    and first he has to train and beat himself
        to stand a chance of defeating his opponent.
    A soldier has to undergo a rigorous training
        if he is to be of any use at all
        when the fighting starts.
Father, if nothing of value can be won in life
    without discipline and self-control,
give me the grace I need to gain self-mastery.
Inspire me during these days
    to run full-out for victory;
    to first pummel my own body
        lest some opponent pummel it;
    to take my share of suffering
        as Christ's loyal soldier should.

A broken and contrite heart

Father, when I look back on my life
    I see in how many ways I have offended you
        and failed to love my fellow men.
I am thankful
    that you never deal with us according to our sins.
As high as the heavens are above the earth,
    such is the height of your unchanging love
        towards those who respect you.
As far as the east is from the west,
    so far do you remove from us our sins.
For you are our gentle and forbearing Father,
    and as a father pities his children,
        so do you, Lord, pity us.
During the solemn season of Lent,
    I specially ask you to create in me a clean heart
        and put a new spirit within me.
Do not cast me from your presence
    nor take your Holy Spirit from me.
It is true, Father, I have often sinned,
    but I pray for a sincere and heart-felt sorrow.
The sacrifice acceptable to you is a broken spirit;
    a broken and contrite heart you will not spurn.
Father, you are the high and lofty One
    who inhabits eternity, whose name is holy.
But Christ came from on high to call sinners like me,
    and he who is our friend assures us
    that you will live in everyone
    who tries to do good to others
        and who has a contrite spirit
            and a humble heart.

I'll start tomorrow

Father, I have a habit of doing today what I want to do
    and putting off what I don't want to do until tomorrow.
I eat heartily today and promise myself
    tomorrow I'll start slimming.
I act ignobly today and promise myself
    tomorrow I'll repent.
But if I cannot add one inch to my height
    or lengthen by one second my span of life
    or turn one of my grey hairs black,
who am I to promise myself
    a thing as doubtful as 'tomorrow'?
My life is but a morning mist;
    it appears for a little while
        then vanishes.
I am like a well-to-do farmer
    whose land was very rich and fertile.
I have so many crops, he said,
    I have nowhere to store them.
I know what I'll do:
tomorrow I'll pull down the barns I own.
Tomorrow I'll start building bigger ones.
I'll store all my grain in them and all my goods.
Then I'll say to my soul,
    Soul, your future is assured.
    Take life easy now. Eat, drink and be merry.
But, Lord, before tomorrow came you whispered in his ear:
    You fool! Tonight I'm taking what is mine: your soul.
    What of your goods tomorrow? Who will inherit them?
Father, help me to be really rich
    by doing what you require of me today.
Help me so to live today that I need not fear
    if tomorrow never comes.

Preparing the soil

Father, Christ the Sower has sown his word in me;
  I pray it will bear fruit a hundred-fold.
But since I know the poor soil of my soul,
  I am afraid no seed will grow in me.
There are unploughed areas of me;
  the seed that falls on them,
  Satan, like a greedy bird, soon gobbles up.
There are shallow and rocky areas of me;
  in these the seed can grow no roots,
  and so, when problems come and hostilities arise,
    it withers in the sun.
There are thorny areas of me;
  in these my heart is full of cares and worldliness,
  and so the seed that falls on them
    is choked and yields no grain.
Father, I pray that through self-discipline,
  I may prepare the soil of my soul
    to receive the seed of Christ your Word.
May it not be said at Eastertide
  that Christ sowed wheat in me
    and only harvested thorns.
Let me, then, weed the ground with abstinence
  plough it with penances
  water it with liberality towards others
and nurture Christ's seed in me
  with prayer that is sincere.
And may you, Father, who supply the Sower with seed
  and who alone can make the wheat-fields grow,
    bring my spirit to a hundred-fold harvest
      that will last throughout eternity.

We always mean what we say

Father, help me to stop using my tongue like a sword.
I say, 'I'm going to give him a piece of my mind,'
  when I should be giving him the whole of my heart.
I say, 'I have to be cruel to be kind,'
  when I am only being cruel to be cruel.
With this tongue I praise you, Lord,
  and wound my brother who is made in your image.
How can this mouth of mine both bless and curse?
Nothing in nature is as unnatural as the tongue.
From a spring there never wells up
  fresh and brackish water.
A fig-tree does not produce olives
  nor a grapevine thorns.
There is no drinking water in the sea.
Why should I alone, Lord, of all the things you made
  be full of contradictions?
Soon after this prayer I will, I know, indulge myself
  in home-truths and half-truths
  in tittle-tattle and insinuations
  in harsh criticism and cynical remarks
  in lading the grapevine
    with another heavy bunch of sour grapes.
Father, you know that often, after speaking unkindly,
  I hastily add, 'I didn't mean it.'
Your Son and perfect Word has solemnly warned us
  that we always mean what we say:
'The mouth only speaks what the heart is full of.
  I tell you when the day of judgement comes
  you will be charged with every thoughtless word
    you have ever said.'

A tongue wagging a man

Father, I know a popular descriptive phrase
    about a tail wagging the dog.
We have all seen a dog so excited it looks
    as if his tail is going to knock him off his feet.
We humans have a similar experience, only, in our case,
    it is our tongue that wags us.
We get so carried away we cannot stop it.
We know that once we start a story, however malicious,
    the listener understandably urges us on:
        You've begun it. You can't stop now!
And human respect compels us to finish the story
    even though it will ruin someone's reputation
        or make a trusting friend into a laughing-stock.
We were wrong to begin the story
    and still more wrong, out of cowardice, to continue it;
but the tongue has wagged us off our feet.
Sometimes, in harmless ways, we wag our tongues;
    it is never harmless when our tongues wag us.
Lord, how humiliating it is that this tiny member
    should have such power over us.
The tongue should be like the rudder of a ship.
The rudder too is very small
    and yet a sea-going ship, driven by boisterous winds,
    goes in the direction the captain decides
        with a mere touch on the helm.
Help me, Father, to be in control of my tongue
    and steer my life on a direct course to you.
Help me, whenever my tongue wants to wag me,
    to give it a good bite first.

Controlling the tongue

Father, help us to master these tongues of ours
  with which we flatter and tease and lie
    and hurt each other.
Indeed, death and life are in the power of the tongue.
The Psalmist is angry with those
  who sharpen their tongues like swords
    and aim deadly words like arrows;
  who shoot from ambush at the blameless,
    firing on them suddenly and without fear.
Wounds inflicted with fists and weapons heal more speedily
  than many wounds inflicted by the tongue.
Father, we know that if we perfectly controlled our tongues
  we would be perfect in every way.
That would mean we had ourselves on a tight rein.
It is easy to put bits into horses' mouths
  and make them do exactly what we want.
The horse is stronger than us, bigger and faster;
  but with that small metal bit
  we turn the horse's head to left or right
    and prove in every way we are its master.
If only, Father, we could ride ourselves as masterfully
  as we ride a horse.
If only our tongues would obey us
  as promptly as a horse with a bit in its mouth.
Father, Jesus said to us,
  'Be perfect as your heavenly Father is perfect.'
You are perfect, heavenly Father,
  because your Word, Jesus Christ, is only truth and love.
Help us gradually to control our tongues so that, in time,
  we may be perfect as you are perfect.

Part VIII

LOVING
ONE ANOTHER
IN CHRIST

The incomprehensible love of Christ

Father, profoundly grateful I come to you
  as your child in Jesus Christ.
You have given me a share
  in the promise of his resurrection.
You have set in my heart
  the burning seal of the Spirit
    as the pledge of the inheritance to come.
Relying on Christ's prayer for me,
  I approach you now as confidently as he.
I bow my knees before you, Father,
  from whom all fatherhood derives.
Strengthen me with might in my inmost self
  through your Holy Spirit
    according to the riches of your glory.
May Christ continue to dwell in my heart through faith
  so that, being rooted and grounded in love,
  I may be able to grasp with all the saints
    what is the breadth and length
    the height and the depth
and to know the love of Christ
  which surpasses all knowledge
so I may be filled with all your fullness, O God.
Through the gift of the Spirit within us,
  you are able to do far more, Father,
    than we can think or ask for.
Strengthened and consoled by the Spirit,
  I give you glory in Christ Jesus
  and in all his disciples
    through all the generations to come.

Love that never changes

Father, it is hard for us to realize
  when we have reached you and pleased you
    and found your forgiveness.
The incessant sacrifices men have offered
  in countless regions and through countless rites
show man's hesitancy in believing
  that you are unchanging in your love.
But Jesus Christ has convinced us that you are our Father:
  you love us when we are good;
  you love us when we are bad.
Christ convinced us when he showed himself to be
  a faithful High Priest,
    holy, blameless, separated from sinners.
He did not need like other priests
  to offer repeated sacrifices for sin.
He sacrificed once and it was enough,
  for what he offered was himself,
    a life that was blameless,
    a death in which your love shone through.
Through his death, Father, you made him perfect for ever,
  and in his love for us
    we saw that you are only love and forgiveness.
From that moment on, sacrifices which have been offered
  since the foundation of the world
    came to an end.
We have been made holy through the offering
  of the body of Jesus Christ,
    once and for all.

Israel's Word of love

Father, I admire the lovely Jewish confession of faith:
'Hear, O Israel, the Lord is God, the Lord is One;
and you shall love the Lord your God with all your heart
    and with all your soul and with all your might.
And these words which I command you this day,
    shall be upon your heart;
and you shall teach them diligently to your children,
and you shall talk of them when you sit in your house,
    and when you walk by the way,
        and when you lie down and when you rise.
And you shall bind them as a sign on your hand
    and they shall be like frontlets between your eyes.
And you shall write them on the doorposts of your house
    and on your gates.'
In Leviticus, it was written:
    'You shall love your neighbour as yourself.'
Even Jesus, Israel's Christ,
    dared not embellish this teaching of his fathers.
A scribe who heard him recite it exclaimed:
    'You are right, Master, in what you have said.
    God is one and there is none but he;
    and to love him with all one's heart
        and mind and strength
    and to love one's neighbour as oneself
        is better than all holocausts and sacrifices.'
Jesus said in reply: 'You are not far from God's kingdom.'
Father, I praise you for your Christ
    in whom your kingdom came
    and who improved on Israel's teaching
        in the only way he could:
        by living it perfectly.

Loving one another

Father, teach us to love one another.
We know that love has its source in you
  as streams have their source in the sea.
We know that whoever loves
  is born of you and knows you.
Father, we cannot doubt your love for us,
  for you sent your Son into the world
    so that in him we might have life.
We did not love you first, Father,
  since there was no love in us then.
No, you loved us first and sent your Son
  so that in him we could see what love was
    and, through love, overcome our faults.
Father, seeing how much you love us, what choice have we
  but to respond by loving one another?
Lord, we follow Christ in calling you 'Father'.
His Spirit within us is prompting us
  to approach you in a childlike way.
We have never seen you, Father,
  except in the flawless mirror of Christ.
And yet when we love each other as Christ loved us,
  we feel that you are living in us
    and your love is opening in us like a flower.
Father, deepen my love of all the people around me,
  my family and friends,
    and all my acquaintances.
Help me to love them by caring for them.
For if I do not love them in this way,
  how can I know you, God,
    who are only and eternally Love?

Putting love first

Father, help me in everything I do to put love first.
If I speak with the tongues of men and angels
   but have not love,
   I am only a noisy gong or a clanging cymbal.
If I have powers of prophecy
   and grasp all mysteries and all knowledge,
and if I have faith so as to lift up mountains,
   but have not love, I am nothing.
If I give away all I have,
   and if I hand my body over to be burned,
   but have not love, I gain nothing.
Love is patient and kind;
   it is not jealous or boastful, coarse or arrogant.
Love is not selfish or irritable or resentful;
it does not rejoice in evil, rather it rejoices in good.
Love bears and believes all things,
   hopes and endures all things.
Love, unlike prophecy or knowledge or the gift of tongues,
   will never pass away,
for knowledge and prophecy, being imperfect, will end;
   while perfect love remains.
When I was a child, Father, I spoke like a child,
   I thought and reasoned like a child.
But having become a man, I put childish ways aside.
Dimly as in a mirror I see now; but then face to face.
In part only I know now; but then I shall understand
   as fully as I am at present understood.
Father, give me abiding faith and hope and love,
   but especially the greatest of them:
      Love.

No greater love

Father, your Son only gave us one commandment:
  that we should love one another as he has loved us.
He showed the greatest possible love
  when he laid down his life for his friends.
This is why, to be his disciples,
  we have to lay down our lives for our brethren.
Father, it is not easy to love everyone.
There are many people who irritate us and dislike us
  and whom we are tempted to dislike in return.
Christ was no stranger to this temptation.
On the cross he was surrounded by people
  who taunted and abused him.
He responded with unswerving love.
He prayed for those who crucified him
  and loved us all right to the end.
It is hard to lay down your life even for good people
  but Jesus gave himself up for us
    when we were sinners and far from good.
With his example to guide us,
  we pray, Father, for all people
    with whom we disagree.
May our prayer be sincere and, if necessary, prolonged
  so as to change our unfriendly heart towards them.
If we exclude any one of them from our love,
  we dwell in a land of death.
We can only be sure we have passed from death to life
  when we love all our brethren,
      as you, Father, love all your children,
        the good and bad alike.

Believing is seeing

Father, after Jesus was risen, the disciples
  did not love him because they saw him;
  they saw him because they loved him.
It was their faith and love
  which opened their eyes so they could see
  that Jesus crucified was really Lord and Christ.
In Jesus' parable of Dives and Lazarus,
  Dives pleads that Lazarus, once so poor,
    be sent from Abraham's bosom
  to warn his five brothers of the burning anguish
    he himself was suffering in Hades.
Abraham said, 'They have Moses and the prophets;
  let them listen to them.'
'No, no, father Abraham,' Dives said.
  'But if someone goes to them risen from the dead
    they will undoubtedly repent.'
To this Abraham replied:
  'If they do not believe Moses and the prophets,
  neither will they be convinced
    if someone rises from the dead.'
Father, the message of Moses and the prophets
  rang out as loudly and clearly as a big bell:
  mercy, justice, love.
If we are stone-deaf to that message
  and Lazarus lies starving at our door,
  how will it help us if Christ himself
    should stand before us in his risen glory?
Father, help us to understand that
  if we do not see Jesus dying in Lazarus,
  we will never know he has been resurrected
    and is alive in our hearts.

Not all fingers and thumbs

Father, teach us to have a profound reverence
  for every human being.
Make us respectful of the young and the old
  the normal and the maladjusted
  the healthy and the disabled
  the wise and the foolish
  the shopkeepers and the shoplifters.
We are all indispensable to each other
  as are the different parts of the body.
If we have no eyes the whole body is blind.
If we have no hearing the whole body is deaf.
If a thumb is crushed the whole body screams.
Every ache, in some sense, is an all-over ache,
  and in every joy the whole of us, body and spirit,
    is lifted up above itself.
But, Father, we are not merely a body of Christians;
  we are the body of Christ.
And in Christ's body there are a number of gifts
  and any number of jobs to be done.
Always, Father, you are the one
  who is the inspiration of them all.
Some of us are priests and religious.
  Some are doctors and nurses.
Some of us are business-men and engineers.
  Some are teachers and students.
Some of us are housewives and mothers.
  Some are retired or handicapped or old.
But we all need each other, Father,
  and we have all received from your Spirit
  the grace to do today the job for the whole body
    that only we can do.

The most beautiful of temples

Father, we are all naturally attached
  to the places where we worship you.
We adorn them and try to keep them in good order.
In them our spirit has grown.
There we find a kind of holy space
  wherein our soul can find repose
  and where we join with others
    in memorable celebrations.
The Psalmist cries exultantly at the temple's beauty:
  'How lovely is your dwelling-place, O Lord of hosts!
  My soul is fainting and longing
    for the courts of the Lord.
  My heart and my flesh sing for joy
    to God, the living God.
  There even a sparrow finds a home
    and the swallow a nest for her brood;
    she lays her young at your altars.
  One day in your courts, O God,
    is preferable to a thousand elsewhere.'
When Jesus was a boy, he, too,
  was lost in wonder at the Temple's loveliness.
But he knew, for all that, Father, that he was greater.
  'Destroy this Temple,' he said;
    then, referring to his body,
  'and in three days I will raise it up.'
Since, Father, we are limbs of Christ's risen body,
  each of us is a temple of the Holy Spirit.
I praise you, Lord, for making every human being,
  however handicapped or misshapen he may be,
    a building more sacred and more beautiful
      than all the temples in the world.

Secret love

Father, make us more generous
   towards people who are worse off than we are.
Sharpen our imagination so we see
   that our contribution, however small,
     can sweeten someone's life,
     if only for an hour.
Christ promises that even a cup of cold water
   given to one of his little ones
     will not go unrewarded.
Father, how hard it is to part with what we have earned
     by the sweat of our brow!
It is like cutting off a part of ourself
   and sharing it among the hungry.
It is, indeed, to become a eucharist
   for feeding others.
And yet, Lord, since we have received freely,
   we ought to give freely in return.
Have you not given us the Comforter
   and Christ our Lord;
and with him everything else besides?
We pray that we may learn to give not grudgingly
   but cheerfully as you have given to us.
May we be magnanimous,
   not wanting to draw attention to ourself
     with a long preparatory trumpet-blast.
Rather, let us give so quietly, so secretly,
   that even our left hand is not aware
     of what our right hand is doing.
Then you, Father, who see in secret
   will generously reward us.

APPENDIX

Table of prayers for Lent and Easter

Many readers may like to use these Bible Prayers in their devotions during the seasons of Lent and Easter. The following table will enable them to have a daily prayer that is in tune with the Church's liturgy from Ash Wednesday to Trinity Sunday.